Art Center College of Design
Library
1700 Lida Street
Pasadena, Calif. 91103

DATE DUE

AUG 0 6 2002		
AUG 1 7 2002		
OCT 2 3 2002		
DEC 1 4 2002		
MAR 0 6 2003		
APR 1 0 2003		
JUI 0 7 2003		
DEC 1 2003		
APR 2 2 2004		
GAYLORD		PRINTED IN U.S.A.

D1442345

ART CENTER COLLEGE OF DESIGN

3 3220 00205 0123

WRIGHT FOR WRIGHT

Other books by Hugh Howard

    The Preservationist's Progress
    How Old Is This House
    Bob Vila's Complete Guide to Remodeling Your Home
    House Dreams

Other books by Roger Straus III

    U. S. 1: America's Original Main Street (with Andrew H. Malcolm)
    Mississippi Currents (with Andrew H. Malcolm)

WRIGHT FOR WRIGHT

Text by Hugh Howard

Photographs by Roger Straus III

Art Center College of Design
Library
1700 Lida Street
Pasadena, Calif. 91103

720.973
W949
H849
2001

Rizzoli
NEW YORK

First published in the United States of America in 2001 by
Rizzoli International Publications, Inc.
300 Park Avenue South
New York, NY 10010

ISBN: 0-8478-2366-0
LC: 00-110875

Copyright © Rizzoli International Publications, Inc.
Photography copyright © 2001 Roger Straus
Text copyright © 2001 Hugh Howard
Designed by Doris Straus

All rights reserved.

No part of this publication may be reproduced in any manner whatsoever
without permission in writing from the publisher.

Distributed by St. Martin's Press

Printed and bound in Hong Kong

CONTENTS

For an accidental modernist, J. Philip Howard

HH

For Doris

R∫

A NOTE ON TITLES AND TIMES

A brief note on names is in order. While in these pages Frank Lloyd Wright will most often be referred to as "Wright" or "Mr. Wright," there are passages where his father or sons are also present. He habitually signed himself FLLW, so in certain contexts those initials are used in order to avoid confusion.

References to the various Taliesins can also become bewildering. For reasons of clarity, Wright's original Taliesin outside of Spring Green, Wisconsin, will be simply "Taliesin" in this volume, though elsewhere in the Wright literature it is known alternatively as "Taliesin North" and "Taliesin East." (More properly, "Taliesin East" refers to Wright's 1954 remodeling of his apartment in New York's Plaza Hotel, occupied while he was at work on the Guggenheim Museum, but that long-demolished suite has no role here.) After the two disastrous fires at Taliesin, Wright himself dubbed the reconstructions "Taliesin II" and "Taliesin III," but for purposes of this book, featuring as it does photographs taken exclusively in the 1990s, "Taliesin" will suffice. In the same way, Taliesin West in Scottsdale, Arizona will be known as just "Taliesin West." Finally, the home Wright built for himself in Oak Park, Illinois has come to be known as the "Home and Studio," thanks to its institutionalization under the aegis of the Frank Lloyd Wright Home and Studio Foundation. We will honor that appellation in these pages although, in thinking of its early history, the reader should keep in mind that it began as a home and that the studio came later.

Wright's Home and Studio, Taliesin, and Taliesin West evolved over a number of decades, meaning that much detective work has been required to date renovations. While scholars have established with some certainty the sequence of changes at each of these sites, this book does not try to recite a building chronology. Rather, as all the images are contemporary, the buildings are described as they stand today, except where other dates are specified.

Arguably Wright's greatest prairie style home – the one he built for himself – Taliesin, near Spring Green, Wisconsin.

INTRODUCTION

The buildings of Frank Lloyd Wright exercise a kind of architectural magic on those who visit them. Even for the serious student of Wright, his works reward repeated examination, as a new appreciation of their complexity and originality is revealed only with familiarity. Yet for many people, the blend of visual elements, dramatic energy, and sheer surprise also produce a sense of puzzlement.

As wonderful as his buildings can be, part of the enigmatic Mr. Wright's legacy is to have left his work wrapped in riddles and mysteries. The sheer volume he produced (some 500 buildings of his design were constructed) and the length of his career (he was active from 1886 to 1959) make understanding Wright difficult.

Though on the grounds of Taliesin, the Unity Chapel is the property of United Chapel, Inc., an independent organization consisting of Lloyd Jones descendants.

One is also distracted by the melodrama that was his personal life, which included a murdered lover, an abandoned first wife and six children, and a life-long flirtation with insolvency. He made good copy and dearly loved the sound of his own voice; the combination of sloppy journalism and suspect recollections further obscure the life.

In his early years, Wright worked anonymously for Louis Sullivan, *der Lieber Meister* (his "beloved master"). The younger architect quickly determined to imprint his personality on his buildings, and he succeeded so well that his fame, voluminous writings, and public pronouncements soon distracted attention from the work. Ever tried examining a house on a foggy day? Little or nothing can be distinguished from a distance and, at close range, hard lines are softened, volumes obscured. Even today, one experiences the same sensation when looking at many Wright buildings. One almost expects the man himself to appear, to explain what one is looking at and, in the process, obfuscate matters in his inimitable manner.

This book attempts to distill a more intimate understanding of Wright's art and philosophy by examining certain core buildings from his diverse oeuvre. The main focus will be on three major works—the Home and Studio, Taliesin, and Taliesin West—with somewhat less detailed detours to roughly a dozen other associated structures. The signal strength of *Wright for Wright* is as obvious as its title: This book will look at the buildings that he designed for himself and members of his family.

In examining the houses Wright built for Wrights (and Lloyd Joneses), his utterances are counterbalanced by a certain purity of intention. Any architect, even one as self-assured and didactic as Wright, has to compromise with the client if he or she wants to stay in business. For Mr. Wright, each commission was to some degree a collaboration that reflected the client's needs, tastes, and budget. The only time an architect has complete aesthetic freedom is when he or she builds for himself or herself (or, perhaps, for a browbeaten relative). Thus, in studying an architect's own homes, one may reach the clearest understanding of that artist's vision. That, at least, is the premise of this undertaking.

Wright for Wright is, by necessity, a mix of biography and autobiography. The dramatic events of Wright's life are inseparable from the story of these buildings. For twenty years, beginning in 1889, he resided in his Oak Park home, living a happy suburban existence with his textbook nuclear family, consisting of Wright, his wife Catherine, and their six children. For the second act, the action moved to Taliesin in Spring Green, Wisconsin, in 1911. The next two decades saw two divorces, the destruction of his home by fire

(twice), and a steep decline in his professional fortunes. In 1938, Wright began building a winter home for himself, Taliesin West, in Scottsdale, Arizona, that was symptomatic of the great creative burst at the end of his life. Until his death in 1959, these cold-weather quarters would accommodate not only Wright and his third wife, Olgivanna, but their much larger family of fellows and apprentices, a coterie of professionals and students that rarely numbered fewer than two or three dozen souls. Each of these three compositions involved at least a home and studio and, in some instances, agricultural, dormitory, theatrical, and other communal buildings.

The Home and Studio, Taliesin, and Taliesin West stand as pivotal points in Wright's long and varied career. They constitute a kind of architectural autobiography—all the important threads of Wright's life and philosophy are interwoven in these diverse buildings which, in turn, represent the major periods in Wright's career. Before we examine the houses, however, a brief summary of the facts of his life is in order.

Wright's father, William Cary Wright, was a widower who had taken a second wife, Anna Lloyd Jones, some ten months before Frank Lincoln Wright was born on June 8, 1867 (his middle name was later changed to

Mature plantings have softened the lines of Taliesin, so much so that imagining the house stripped of its vegetative texture is almost impossible.

Lloyd). The birthing took place in Richland Center, Wisconsin. In 1869 and 1877, respectively, sisters Many Jane (usually called "Jane") and Margaret Ellen ("Maginel") joined the family.

The women in the household would prove to be a continuing presence in Wright's life. In his later writings, however, he dismissed his father, although William C. Wright was a man of many accomplishments. He was a sometime lawyer, clergyman, teacher, musician, politician, and orator whose eulogy to Lincoln on the courthouse lawn in Richland Center may have been one factor in the choice of his son's original middle name. As his multiple careers might suggest, William Wright was a man for whom change seemed to have a continuing attraction, and Wright's childhood was an itinerant one, as the family moved from Wisconsin to McGregor, Iowa, before Wright turned two; to Pawtucket, Rhode Island, in 1871; and to Weymouth, Massachusetts, in 1875.

In later writings, Wright's memories seem to have begun during the three years spent in Weymouth. As early architectural memories tend to do, his recollections of his home there, the "modest, gray wooden house," probably informed some of his early designs. Perhaps just as important, the Weymouth years were also the time when, according to Wright, his mother traveled to the Philadelphia Centennial Exposition and returned with the Froebel gifts.

German educator Friedrich Froebel (1782-1852) has been tagged the "father of the kindergarten" (literally, "children's garden"). His notion was to develop the intelligence of children by engaging them in various object lessons, games, song, and play. In particular, he prescribed special toys of his own devising. By the 1870s, Milton Bradley, then a lithographer of entrepreneurial inclination, was manufacturing the toys in the United States.

The sky, the mountains, and Taliesin West melding in the desert heat.

Froebel's Gifts and Occupations, as they were formally known, were more than mere buildings blocks. They constituted nothing less than a series of exercises in color and space. Presented to a child sequentially, the gifts began with a sphere, cylinder, and cube. Smaller cubes followed, then slats and rings, leading to three-dimensional experiments using sticks for lines and peas or wax pellets to represent points (Buckminster Fuller traced his invention of the triangulated geodesic dome structure to kindergarten play with the Gifts). According to Froebel, the Gifts and Occupations were to teach a child to build "forms of life" (structures, trees, furniture) and to represent "forms of knowledge" (giving physical form to abstract ideas like geometry), eventually moving to the creation of "forms of beauty." Froebel's toys were intended to exercise the imagination and to teach aesthetics (symmetry was fundamental to the approach), all the while encouraging a child to do what many children love most to do, manipulate objects in a quasi-independent fashion.

Wright certainly played with the Froebel Gifts as a child and, much later as a man, talked of their influence ("A small interior world of color and form [came] within the grasp of my little fingers"). Whether his mother "discovered" them at the Centennial Exposition is open to dispute, as is the often-made assertion that her programmatic mothering predestined him to become an architect (she hung engravings of cathedrals in the nursery when Wright was a baby). But many of Wright's recollections contradict known facts. His personal history is a fit subject for analysis, both psychological and historiographical. The apocryphal role Wright assigned the Froebel Gifts and Occupations symbolized his penchant for mingling convenient and unverifiable fictions in recounting the facts of his life.

Wright's rejection of his father was also disingenuous. Perhaps Wright was simply afraid to look in the family mirror—or his domineering mother forbade him to do so—because the fatherly reflection he would see

there would be of a man more than a little like himself, of short physical stature but with a compelling public presence, a man with a passion for the arts (in particular, music), a man whose financial incompetence presaged Wright the spendthrift. The resemblances between Frank Lloyd and William Carey Wright are many.

Yet Wright's distortions often reveal as much as they obscure. In the case of the blocks, they are a convenient metaphor. The Froebel Gifts symbolize something of what made Wright special. Wright managed to reinvent himself throughout his career—as the houses here, as well as his larger body of work, demonstrate. Unlike most people, he maintained a sense of play throughout his life, an openness to experimentation, to taking chances. Whether Friedrich Froebel gets a little or a lot of credit for nurturing the lifelong child in Wright can never be resolved; that some of the essential freedom of childhood remained with Wright is beyond dispute.

The family returned to Wisconsin in 1878 and initially resided with his mother's family, the Lloyd Joneses. The switch of his middle name from Lincoln to Lloyd had come earlier, but the influence of the Lloyd Jones clan truly began to be felt in the Wisconsin years.

Anna Lloyd Jones, the child of Welsh immigrants, had arrived with her family in Wisconsin in 1845.

At the Home and Studio, geometric experimentation was always the order of the day.

By the mid-1850s, the family had grown (Anna was one of eleven children) and had settled permanently in the farming village of Hillside, just across the Wisconsin River from the town of Spring Green. In the Helena Valley, the God-fearing, disciplined family prospered and their stability was a sharp contrast to the nomadic life the family of William Wright had lived. By age eleven, young FLLW found himself spending his summers working the land, shoulder to shoulder with his burly and bearded uncles, in particular Uncle James. During those summers, Wright experienced something akin to a religious conversion. Though secular in kind, the affinity that Wright developed for nature in general and that valley in particular would be at the core of his philosophy and sense of belonging for the next eight decades. There was a tenuous balance between the respect he developed for the rigor and discipline of the Lloyd Jones clan on one hand, and the awe he felt for the beauty, fertility, and order of the natural world from which they drew their existence on the other.

Anna's brother, Jenkin Lloyd Jones, an influential Unitarian clergyman in Chicago and secretary of the Western Unitarian Conference, found a position for William Wright in nearby Wyoming, Wisconsin. For the next few years, the Wright family lived in Madison, where Wright attended public schools before moving on to the University of Wisconsin. His family life changed radically during this time, as his parents divorced in 1885. Wright left school to work in an architectural office, but it was the Lloyd Joneses who, once again, provided the stability—and the opportunity—that would be the stepping-off point for Wright's nascent architectural career.

The homey Unity Chapel was that opportunity. This meetinghouse, intended to be both a house of worship and a gathering place for the Lloyd Joneses and their neighbors, was anticipated not by a structure but by a stand of pine trees. The family had held what they called "Grove Meetings," annual ceremonies to celebrate the harvest, which were conducted in the towering, cathedral-like space beneath a canopy of evergreens. Given Wright's later philosophy of "organic architecture," a more fitting antecedent for this, the first building he helped design, could hardly be imagined.

Commissioned in 1886 by several Lloyd Jones aunts and uncles, the Unity Chapel was nominally the work of Joseph Lyman Silsbee, a Chicago architect who had designed a church for Uncle Jenkin the previous year. While Wright played some role in the chapel's design, distinguishing his contributions from Silsbee's is impossible, even though a perspective drawing in Wright's hand survives, bearing the signature "F.L. Wright, Del[ineator]." On the basis of that sketch and a passing mention in a church publication ("a boy architect belonging to the family looked after the interior"), the church is usually cited as Opus 1 in the Works of Wright.

The Unity Chapel also helped establish an early and important professional bond. There was an implied collaboration between the accomplished Silsbee and the nineteen-year-old Wright which emboldened the latter to depart for Chicago early in 1887 to work in Silsbee's office. While working there, Wright may well have felt the first stirring of what would prove to be a life-long passion for residential architecture, and echoes of Silsbee's architectural style would be apparent in Wright's Oak Park home two years later. Wright also had his first encounter with Japanese prints in Silsbee's office, as the walls were decorated with art provided by Silsbee's cousin, the orientalist Ernest Francisco Fenollosa.

The Unity Chapel commission helped launch Wright's career; it also remained in his personal landscape throughout his life. During his first marriage, he traveled often to Spring Green, designing buildings for other members of the Lloyd Jones clan. Later, he built for himself the manorial Taliesin, from which the bell tower of the chapel could be glimpsed in the valley below. Late in life Wright routinely preached in the chapel, offering lay sermons that characteristically had less relation to matters of theology than to Wright's personal philosophizing (the chapel, thanks to Uncle Jenkin, had traditionally been nondenominational, its pulpit open to laymen and preachers alike). Wright's funeral eulogy was read in the chapel to some two hundred denizens of Taliesin and Spring Green, after which he was buried in the nearby family cemetery. Before we bury him, however, let us revisit moments of his life and some of his works which, in a sense, began and ended at the Unity Chapel. Almost certainly it was there that he recognized architecture as his true calling.

The array of geometric masses that is the *Studio* almost obscures the earlier Home to the rear with its steeply pitched gables. While not exactly a unified whole, this complex of structures clearly conveys big ideas were born here.

I The HOME and STUDIO
Oak Park, Illinois

At first glance, the residence at 428 Forest Avenue hardly looks like a seminal work of an architectural revolutionary. Numerous other houses in fashionable Oak Park, many of them later works by Wright himself, are more unexpected, evoking admiring or even dismayed responses from passersby. Yet Frank Lloyd Wright's 1889 home, as well as the more startling studio he grafted onto it nine years later, was the site of heady experimentation for two decades.

Wright had arrived in Chicago in 1887 to work for Silsbee. The following year he moved on to the employ of Adler & Sullivan, where Wright quickly distinguished himself in the eyes of Sullivan and his partner,

The shingle style evolved from the eclectic and elaborate Queen Anne. While the typical shingle style house was distinguished from other nineteenth-century styles by its simplified surfaces and volumes, Wright went one step further, seeking to extract some geometric truth. Pure shapes are apparent in looking at its exterior, in particular the tall triangle of the gable. Note, too, the veranda with its brick parapet that seems seemed to anchor the house to the ground.

Dankmar Adler. He quite literally became Sullivan's right-hand man, as Wright's office was an anteroom immediately adjoining Sullivan's, a place of prominence and access. Wright himself termed his role "the pencil in Sullivan's hand."

When Wright went to work for Sullivan, he was twenty years old. Sullivan was only thirty-one but was already an accomplished architect. Having studied at the Massachusetts Institute of Technology and at the Ecole des Beaux-Arts in Paris, Sullivan had a diverse education that contrasted with Wright's. The younger man had had only two semesters of engineering training at the University of Wisconsin and even less time under Silsbee's tutelage. The five years he would spend at Adler & Sullivan would prove to be his apprenticeship, the architectural grounding he needed to launch himself on his own. The pragmatic Adler, a skilled engineer, and the imaginative Sullivan, a gifted artist, proved excellent tutors.

Wright's debt to Sullivan in particular was more than that of a disciple to a generous mentor. He missed nothing from his vantage at the side of the master. Wright became Sullivan's trusted friend and confidant, a relationship based not only on architecture but also on their shared enthusiasms for music and books. Working for Sullivan, Wright mastered the biomorphic detailing (nature-inspired ornamentation) so characteristic of Sullivan's work and, later, of some of Wright's prairie style buildings. Ironically, the older man's indifference to designing houses was key in giving Wright his chance.

He proved so apt a pupil that almost from the start Wright was assigned the residential work that came into the firm. Even after Wright's departure from the practice Sullivan completed only two residential commissions prior to his death in 1924, so he easily fell into the habit of handing the residential jobs over to the man who had quickly become his head draftsman. If Silsbee whetted Wright's appetite for domestic architecture, then Sullivan gave him the opportunity to try it as a steady diet. He clearly found it to his liking because today, despite a number of major industrial, civic, and ecclesiastical designs, Wright is most often admired for his houses.

Wright's Oak Park home is identifiable as an early work of his in many ways, but perhaps none is so obvious as the positioning of the front door. Here it's very much to the fore; later it would became a virtual compulsion to conceal the entrance to his houses.

Wright owed a great deal to Sullivan: the man was his employer, teacher, mentor, friend, and, ironically, eventual liberator when, in 1893, he dismissed Wright from the firm. But four years prior to that Sullivan had also agreed to be Wright's banker, loaning him $5,000 to buy a lot and to build a house for himself and his betrothed. That house was to be the first of hundreds he would design and is a kind of skeleton key to how Wright helped move American architecture out of the Victorian age.

The original Oak Park house reflects the domesticated Wright, the father and husband, living the American dream on a staid residential street a comfortable distance from the energy of Chicago. In a way that neither Taliesin nor Taliesin West does, the Oak Park home also suggests the influence of the woman in his life.

At the time he designed, built, and almost immediately began to renovate the Oak Park home, he and Catherine Tobin were newlyweds. They were both young (he was just twenty-one when they married in June of 1889), but he brought to the making of their home his precocious talent for buildings, as well as an unpol-

The lush plantings around the house were from the start essential to Wright's vision of his home.

Upon entering, the visitor to the home was met by classical sculpture (the Venus de Milo was Wright's favorite) and stylized trimwork in naturally finished oak.

ished charm, a charismatic quality that later came to be thought of as an expression of his genius. Her contributions to their home life included a degree of practicality surprising in an eighteen-year-old bride.

Catherine was the one who insisted they save money; she helped manage their finances, a skill that the profligate Wright never came close to mastering. She had grown up in prosperous circumstances, the daughter of a Chicago businessman. Both Wright and the red-haired Catherine were inexperienced sexually when they married (she was the only girl he had ever kissed); their union produced six children and, before Wright began to wander, they made a fine team. She was well practiced in negotiating the social conventions that were foreign to her husband. She moved easily in the upper-middle-class milieu whence architectural commissions came. Many early clients were urbanites and suburbanites of means, people with rather different social aspirations from the farming stock he knew in his mother's family and from his itinerant preacher-musician father. The social niceties Catherine mastered in her childhood home proved invaluable in helping Wright mature and adapt to his new world. While Catherine probably had little direct impact upon the design of the house, and she

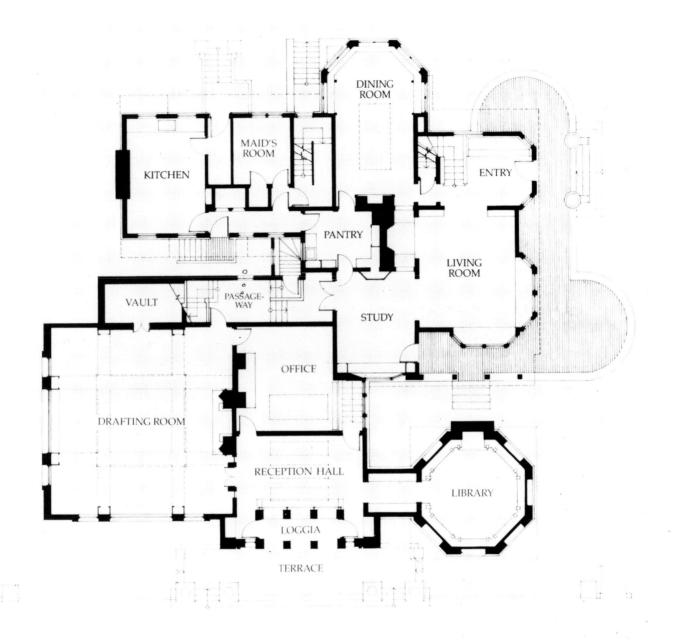

The floor plan of the Home and Studio, 1898 and after.

was soon heard to complain that Wright was more interested in it than in her and the family, she and the anticipated children did play a crucial role in establishing the original program.

By the standards of his later work, the dwelling they moved into in 1889 on Forest Avenue was fashionable but not particularly forward-looking. It was an example of the relatively new shingle style, as in it
Wright revisited the work of his first mentor, Joseph Lyman Silsbee. He gave it his own spin, however, and in
retrospect one can distinguish elements common in Wright's later work, such as the modified Palladian window on the front façade with its six sections (eliminate the lunette window on top and what's left is a ribbon
of windows characteristic of the prairie style). But the original house, with its boxy shape and sweeping roof,
was little more than a modest reworking of what were rapidly becoming vernacular themes. For a decade, the
likes of Bruce Price and the firm of McKim, Mead & White on the eastern seaboard had been building similar homes in a style originally referred to as "seaside" because of the settings. Silsbee himself had moved to
Chicago from the east coast, bringing the shingle style with him. Wright's Oak Park home was a recogniza-

At once, it's a Colonial Revival space (note the lozenge casements) with a Victorian feel (thanks to the plants and the bays), but it's vintage Wright with the windows that sweep around the corner.

ble member of that fraternity of casual cottages.

The outsized roof dominated the front elevation of the original house. Its design may have been inspired by a Tuxedo Park house by Bruce Price, which was published three years before the construction of Wright's home, or by Charles Follen McKim's thrilling Low House, that landmark of the shingle style with its immensely broad gable. Yet the sources for Wright's design are less important than the ways in which Wright manipulated them over a period of twenty years.

Visiting the home today, one does not sense the aura of Wright's recent departure; rather, there are the echoing footsteps of the preceding group of tourists. Wright fled his marriage and Oak Park life in 1909, the time to which the place has been restored by the National Trust for

It's a vernacular Victorian interior with a difference: note the characteristic built-ins, in this case the sofas in the bay.

Historic Preservation, which owns the home, and The Frank Lloyd Wright Home and Studio Foundation, which administers it. Despite the evidence of the 75,000 people admitted annually, there is an invigorating sense of time travel, of following Wright through his early years of development. The visitor is a voyager taken on a walk through time, beginning in Wright's starter house, designed by a very young man, little more than an apprentice, for his wife and children. There is an 1895 addition at the rear of the home, as well as the later studio. On the tour the visitor can bear witness to the ways in which the visionary architect departed from his earlier influences. A century ago, a guest of Wright's would have traveled to the future, but today's tourists look back upon the first major flowering of his genius.

Today Oak Park is a tightly packed suburban grid, but when Wright built his home there it was sparsely settled. Forest Avenue, one of the earliest residential streets in Oak Park, was paved the year the house was built. The lot Wright purchased was woodsy and his siting of the house, nestled into dense vegetation, anticipated his organic architecture, a subject on which he would discourse at length later in life. As was often the case, however, Wright wasn't opposed to improvements made upon the work of Mother Nature. The corner plot at Forest and Chicago Avenues had been a nursery for a Scottish landscape gardener working in the vicinity, so its mature plantings included specimens of both native and exotic species. The immediate setting was a stark contrast to the landscape across the dirt byway that was Chicago Avenue. There the view was of an undeveloped expanse of open prairie.

The tall, spindleback chairs stand at attention around the table, defining and differentiating the eating area from the service spaces on the periphery.

In his autobiography Wright remembered that the lot was purchased for $1,500, leaving him with $3,500 to build the house. In true Wright style, construction costs overran his budget by more than a third.

The interior of the house can be read as a series of variations on earlier themes. There were six principal rooms in the original home, three up and three down. The front door led to an entry hall featuring the stair to the second floor and an opening to the living room. Consistent with many earlier shingle style houses, the rectangular portal was large, as were those from the living room to the inglenook and to the dining room. The living room also featured Queen Anne bay windows (one was original, the other added in the 1895 remodeling). Such bays had become vernacular by 1889, but Wright's placement of the pair was unusual and presaged his later use of corner windows. The two bay windows wrapping around the corner produced a panoramic view.

The ceiling illumination in the dining room is generally regarded as the first example of recessed lighting with its stylized decorative fretwork of oak branches and leaves. Wright was always quick to adopt new technologies and recessing lights into a panel in this way was newly possible thanks to electric lights. The house had been wired for electricity at the time of construction (Wright had first-hand knowledge of electrical service from his work at Adler and Sullivan) and the arrival of municipal power in Oak Park in 1891 made wiring such fixtures a simple matter.

The playroom was a true multipurpose room and the child's toys, built-in book cases, large fireplace, and other elements suggest some of its uses. The mural illustrates the allegory of the Fisherman and Genii from the *Arabian Nights*.

The ground floor also featured a kitchen and dining room to the rear; upstairs was the master bedroom, a nursery, the only bathroom, and a generous studio that Wright used for his *ex-officio* practice.

By all accounts, this was a happy home for Frank and Catherine, affectionately known as Kitty. The first months of their marriage had been spent next door in a house owned by Wright's mother, Anna Wright, who took no pains to keep her hostility toward her new daughter-in-law to herself. "Poor Kitty," remembered Maginel Wright Barney many years later, "she didn't deserve so forcible an adversary as my mother." But once they moved into their home, Kitty came into her own.

The house was initially decorated with auction finds. Saturday night sales would be followed by Sundays spent rearranging the furniture to accommodate new discoveries. There were Greek sculpture, oriental rugs, Japanese silk paintings, and a Jacobean chest. As Wright experienced his house and consequently rethought its spaces and details, he added built-ins like the window seats in the living room and various cabinets. This was a practice Wright would return to again and again. But his home was an eclectic place with its share of Victorian touches, including fabric portieres and oversized plants. And, not least, the hearth.

The focus of the living room—in fact, of the whole house—was the inglenook. Early in the Victorian age, the functional fireplace had gone out of favor, as for some years around mid-century most houses were built not with colonial fireplaces but with stove chimneys that had efficient cast-iron stoves plugged into them. Yet the fireplace quickly made a comeback, becoming associated in the public consciousness with notions of domestic life. In simple terms, the ideas of home and hearth became inseparable and Wright, like most of us, felt an atavistic attraction to an open fire. He was a child of the Victorian age but fire also suited the philosophical underpinnings he evolved for his art, as he liked to say he worked with air, water, earth, and fire. Appropriately, then, Wright planted a monolithic masonry mass at the very heart of this, his first domestic design. For him, the vestigial appeal of fire never faded, and the sight of open flames and the smell of wood

The north gable end of the master bed-room featured a mural of Orlando Giannini, a sometime collaborator of Wright's who was also an illustrator and art glass designer. Though the mural is said to depict Native Americans, the garb seems rather Egyptian, an allusion enhanced by the amphora-shaped lights. The mural reemerged during the restoration of the Home and Studio in the 1980s from beneath ten layers of paint.

In stringing seven art-glass windows together into this bay window Wright managed both to open the playroom room to the outdoors yet also to screen off the view outside.

smoke were sensory pleasures he offered to virtually all the clients who commissioned him to build homes.

While fireplaces in general became basic to Wright's architectural grammar, the inglenook treatment in the Oak Park home was inspired by a then-current vogue in intimate spaces based upon English tastes of the time. But Wright could easily rationalize the inclusion. The word "inglenook" is Welsh for "flame corner" and thus, for Wright, this was a bow to the ancestry of his mother and his uncles. It should not go unrecorded as well that, consciously or not, the chimney stack–like the modest early New England houses Wright encountered at the dawn of his architectural consciousness–is at the core of the house. The masonry is of Roman brick, another often-seen element in Wright's work. The use of family mottoes heralded Wright's life-long penchant for aphorisms.

Is the inglenook a successful space? Not really. It is formal, rigidly symmetrical, and too small for the firebox. A crackling fire of the sort Wright liked to talk about overwhelmed the volume of the space, making it too hot to sit in comfortably. In truth, the inglenook is more symbolic of warmth and togetherness. But then, as time would show, so was Wright's commitment to his family.

Upon leaving the inglenook and the living room, the floor plan flows continuously around the ground floor. Wide portals provide a sense of openness to the interior, in contrast to the way the exterior is closed off, the house set back on the property into the dense plantings. Perhaps a metaphorical circling of the wagons filled an emotional need of Wright's; after all, he built this home for his newly established nuclear unit only four years after his parents' divorce. Yet Wright never ceased changing things as, over the next decade, the place would become a laboratory for his architectural experiments.

Wright and Catherine's first child, Frank Lloyd Wright, Jr. (later shortened to Lloyd Wright), was born in March 1890. He was followed by John in 1892, Catherine in 1894, David in 1895, Frances in 1898, and Robert

Art Center College of Design
Library
1700 Lida Street
Pasadena, Calif. 91103

From the sidewalk, the Studio–pictured here as restored to its circa 1909 appearance–featured numerous decorative elements, including sculptures executed by one of Wright's collaborators at the time, Richard Bock. Two male sculptures called "The Boulders" crouch like buttresses, while below, in a fanciful arcade, storks look out from the piers with a scroll of architectural plans between each pair. The finely wrought storks are an act of homage to Louis Sullivan.

Llewellyn in 1903. His growing brood forced Wright to enlarge the house and in 1895 he added a wing to the rear and east of the original structure, a renovation that also involved rearranging several existing rooms. This effectively doubled the size of the home, expanding its floor space to almost 3,600 square feet.

The addition to the house became less Victorian as Wright tried out more ideas of his own. On the interior, this house-as-laboratory tendency was particularly apparent. Many motifs characteristic of Wright's work in the Oak Park period and after made early appearances here. Art-glass windows, site-specific furniture, and recessed lighting were among the elements with which he experimented.

The 1895 renovation added two truly memorable rooms to the house, a dining room downstairs and a playroom on the upper level.

The new dining room was located where the old kitchen had been, though the addition of a bay window to the south roughly doubled its area. The room is perhaps Wright's first assay in composing all the elements of a space. The structure, including the lowered ceiling with its recessed lighting, the art-glass windows, the interior finish, the built-ins, and even the free-standing furniture were designed of-a-piece.

In the 1890s, a dinner party was bound by conventions. There were established rituals to be obeyed. An air of formality dominated the proceedings, a carefully choreographed sequence involving food and drink served according to a meticulous plan by servants (the Wrights had two). Catherine Wright was a well-schooled hostess and she educated Wright early in their marriage about the social expectations of a formal dinner party. Having given and attended many such parties in the intervening years, Wright had by 1895 developed his own notions of how to create a dining space that conveyed a sense of order and intimacy.

The dining room at Oak Park has a calm, serene quality that is in part a consequence of careful composition, as the room is a symmetrical arrangement of geometric shapes. The color scheme is somber, of earthy browns and natural wood finishes. Yet the room is memorable because of the tall, straight-backed chairs, notably uncomfortable though they are, which seem to enclose the table, establishing what Wright called a "room within a room." Adding to the effect is the recessed lighting above, with its fretwork ceiling grille. There is nothing haphazard about this room: Wright was in absolute control.

If the programmatic demands of a dining room made it the perfect place for exercising such mastery, the playroom was a place for less inhibited experimentation. Although designed early in his career, the room remains high on the list of Wright's great spaces. It is a pleasing mix of illusion (it is smaller than it seems), an enchanting space, playful, warm, and dramatic. Here again, the playroom represents a significant advance for Wright in moving from a vernacular Victorian interior to a space that we now recognize as distinctly Wrightian.

Wright earned the reputation for building houses his way, turning the old aphorism "the customer is always right" on its ear. Catherine was perhaps the first object of his the-architect-knows-best philosophy. She

True, there was but one bathroom in the house to serve the entire family, but then indoor bathrooms were still the exception in 1889. This one was handsome indeed, with horizontal, board-and-batten oak walls, maple flooring, a marble sink surround, and nickel-plated fittings. Another unusual aspect is the light well behind the sink. The opening in the wall had originally been a window, but the playroom had been added to that elevation. Wright's solution was to add a small projecting bay and to shift the window ninety degrees. The result is light, ventilation, and an added sense of privacy.

may have wanted more bedrooms for their growing family; instead, Wright built the playroom as the first of his grand theatrical spaces.

Kitty gave kindergarten classes there, initially for her children, and later for neighborhood youngsters as well. But Wright didn't build the grand playroom space solely to function as a kindergarten. This was a grand—and successful—spatial experiment that anticipated many elements of Wright's greatest early buildings, especially in its detailing (the ribbed arches) and use of natural materials (wood and brick). The playroom revealed for the first time Wright's skill with a barrel vault. The vault is fifteen feet high and eighteen feet wide (the child-height knee walls, at 5 1/2 feet tall, make it seem higher). It anticipates the gallery in the Dana House (another multiuse, public space) and the theaters at the Taliesins.

If this was officially a play space for the *kinder*, it was an aspirational space, too. Wright was ever conscious of "the sell," and he frequently entertained clients there so they could take the measure of his skill at rethinking domestic spaces. This was also the room where Wright put his player piano. He loved performance, both musical and theatrical, and this playroom afforded adults, as well as children, the opportunity to enjoy themselves. Wright played the piano; his children all played instruments, typically with cello-playing son Lloyd conducting the ensemble. Thus, the playroom was a gymnasium, recital hall, theater, and kindergarten, as well as architectural statement, especially when contrasted to the modest living room downstairs.

While the home and studio abut one another, this is no Siamese-twin. Aside from a few common horizontals visible from the west elevation, Wright made little attempt to match the studio to the house; one was a workplace, one a home and he disliked when his home life interrupted his business. Even their official orientation to the world is different: the house faces Forest Avenue, a sedate residential street, while the studio looks out onto Chicago Avenue, the Illinois equivalent of a Roman road, a vector bound straight for Chicago.

Other changes were made in the house at the time the new dining room and the playroom were added. Beneath was a new kitchen, largely the maid's province, with its iron cookstove and wooden ice box. A pantry and maid's room were also incorporated in the 1895 remodeling. The old dining room was converted to a study where the children did their homework.

Hidden just inside the ends of the loggia are two doorways.

Wright's drafting room is not only vertical with a roof that is effectively three stories above the floor level. The horizontals also define the space, with the long window and the suspended shelf above distinguishing the lower level from the tall octagonal drum above. To supplement natural light, general illumination was provided by Holophane spheres and task lighting by lights in the green glass shades.

Perhaps surprisingly in a home with four children, no new bedroom was added. Earlier, after he had established independent offices in Chicago following his departure from Adler & Sullivan, Wright had converted his studio into a sort of barracks, with one room for girls and one for boys. A low partition wall was added, leaving a shared, tall ceiling. This aided ventilation and added a grander sense of space, as well as making possible the fondly remembered pillow-tossing contests from one side to the other. The original children's room became Catherine's day room, a place for her to sew and read.

The master bedroom was another careful composition of disparate elements. A ribbed ceiling reminiscent of the overhead poles in an Indian wigwam framed gable ends that featured murals depicting American plains Indians. Beneath the vaulted ceiling, the tops of the walls were defined by a stenciled frieze derived from the decorations used in the Auditorium Theater, the great Sullivan design with which Wright assisted when first employed at Adler & Sullivan. The assemblage of tall elements helped give the modest-sized room a more spacious feel. Wright also designed the bed and assembled a pair of doors and two windows into a T-shape that provided access to a small balcony.

As charming and appealing as were the spaces in this house, all was not familial bliss. Wright resented the expense of the children. Catherine and the children were sensitive to his immersion in work to the exclusion of his family. Bill collectors came and one even spent a night in the playroom, waiting to collect $85.00

overdue for its construction. Wright himself described his progeny as "their mother's children." Of himself and the notion of fatherhood he said, "I am afraid I never looked the part. Nor ever acted it. I didn't feel it. And I didn't know how."

In 1893 Louis Sullivan learned that Wright was moonlighting, designing a series of what Wright himself termed "bootleg" houses for his neighbors in Oak Park. This was an explicit violation of his terms of employment, and Wright was dismissed from the firm. His firing only hastened the inevitable—Wright was not destined to be anyone's second for very long—and he seized the opportunity.

He rented office space in downtown Chicago with other architects and, for five years, built his business there, nine miles east of Oak Park. From various addresses, the practice flourished. By 1898, he had determined to move his practice home, establishing what would be a life-long pattern of living and working under the same roof. To accommodate his needs and those of a growing circle of architects and artisans around him, he undertook construction of a studio. The addition of approximately 2,500 square feet brought the area of the combined home and office to almost 6,200 square feet.

If the house to which the studio was attached was to some degree in synchrony with its context–a neighborhood of late Victorian houses in the Queen Anne, stick, and Italianate styles–then the studio most certainly was not. Its appearance was so distinct that the neighbors, for lack of a more familiar stylistic term, took to referring to it as "that strange building with the tree growing through it." The reference was to a willow tree that, before construction, had been growing in the proposed site of the connecting corridor between the new studio and the house. Rather than chop it down, Wright built around it, the first but not the last time he would use the celebrated trick of incorporating a living tree into his design.

The studio was in stark contrast to the house. While the house would surprise few passersby, the studio no doubt turned many heads. A potential client consulting with Wright there was met with what we now recognize as Wright's characteristic blending of showmanship and salesmanship. The visitor approached a set of buildings of varying heights and shapes. The simple box had been banished, replaced by a small octagon at one corner and a larger one at the other. (The seesaw effect of two masses flanking a smaller, central link was a motif he would use again and again at such commissions as the Hillside Home School and the Unity Temple). The insightful onlooker could also read into the masses much about the volumes on the inside, but this

The inglenook as a whole alludes to the English Arts and Crafts movement; the arched opening around the fire box recalls the work of both of Wright's mentors, Silsbee and Sullivan.

Wright designed the furnishings in the room, including the drafting tables with their hard maple work surfaces and darker bases.

was not a building to be absorbed all in a glance.

There was no one façade. The multiple planes of the octagons flanked an entrance in the middle that was largely hidden behind a low brick wall decorated with urns overflowing with vegetation (such stone urns were another decorative motif of Wright's that he would utilize in many of his designs). The complexity of the elements also helped obscure the inexpensive materials: common brick and cedar. To the neighbors, it must have seemed a shocking agglomeration, but it didn't broadcast the fact that it was commercial space (though more than one wag observed that the whole building was an advertisement for Wright's work). The identity of the place was evident only because of a limestone panel inset on the brick walling into which was carved Wright's name and profession. The entrance itself was not apparent (another lifelong technique of Wright's), obscured as it was in a stylized loggia several steps above the level of Chicago Avenue.

Like his later and even bolder prairie houses in Oak Park, the studio does not blend into the streetscape. Wright had begun to practice what he would later preach, melding his architecture not so much into the context of the built environment but into its organic setting, the terrain, vegetation, the topography of its context. His mastery of his own sense of geometry and detailing was emerging.

Although he was no longer employed by an architectural firm, Wright in his Oak Park days had many important collaborators. These disciples—some were more senior than others, but none truly his peer—served informal apprenticeships at what Wright would call "our little university." They looked to their youthful mentor (Wright turned twenty-six the year he left Adler & Sullivan) for both inspiration and work. Wright, in turn, gave them considerable creative freedom and credit (unlike later in his career, when he kept the contributions of those around him largely anonymous).

At his Oak Park studio, he had the benefit of such collaborators as Walter Burley Griffin, later an independent architect of international note, and Marion Mahony, a gifted artist whose drawings surely helped Wright attract business. Sculptor Richard Bock and painter Orlando Giannini were there. There were other architects, too, some of whom continued to work independently in the prairie style even after Wright had moved on, including George Elmslie and William Drummond. Truly, if the prairie "school" ever had an address, it was 951 Chicago Avenue, Wright's Oak Park studio. The prairie school was developed there and scholars believe that

In the studio library, Wright's clients would be greeted with drawings, either pinned onto the vertical cork panels around the perimeter of the room or spread on the table. This was both a private, intimate place to plan a future home and a highly detailed model interior suggestive of the emerging Wright style.

some 140 executed designs were produced by Wright and his colleagues within its walls. In the long term, the studio would also prove to have been a dress rehearsal for the later Taliesin Fellowship.

Entering the studio, the visitor was at the mercy of Mr. Wright and his predilection for the unexpected. Throughout his career Wright liked nothing better than to surprise people. To enter the studio, the visitor had to navigate a virtual maze, turning no fewer than five times to reach the reception hall. Once there, the visitor had three options: straight ahead was Mr. Wright's office, to the right the library, and to the left the drafting room.

His office was similar in scale to the reception hall. Both spaces have art-glass ceiling panels and relatively low ceilings. Natural light, filtered through the greens and golds of the art glass, reflects off the gold-painted walls, framed by the dark-stained wood trim. These low, rather severe and somber spaces set the visitor up for one of Wright's favorite manipulations: the low-ceiling spaces give way to the vast and sunlit openness of the drafting room to the east. Wright himself was not tall; his father had been very short and FLLW, though his passport listed him as being five feet, eight and a half inches tall, was closer to five feet, six inches. He was known to wear built-up heels and, while his proud carriage helped give the illusion of taller stature, he was not above instructing his rangy son-in-law Wes Peters, a long-time Taliesin fellow, to sit down because he was throwing everything out of scale. Wright's self-consciousness about his height may have played a role in his frequent variations in ceiling heights.

With so much going on, it's not surprising that the Studio from some angles has a confusing profusion of shapes and decorations.

There is a complex interplay of geometric shapes in the drafting room, too, with a square first floor that is topped by an octagonal mezzanine. The windows are high on the wall, so the visitor is undistracted by exterior views and the light is diffused. The mezzanine is suspended like a catwalk from a network of iron chains that are held in tension by a smaller octagonal ring of chains. This clever system both holds up the mezzanine and strengthens the building envelope, holding the roof and walls in place like a set of collar ties.

The result was a showy space, a fit setting for a wedding (both Wright's sisters, Maginel and Jane, were married there). But it was a practical room, too, where six or more apprentices could work at first-floor drafting tables while artists designed sculpture and art glass on the balcony above. As always with Wright, there was an eclectic array of objects for admiration and inspiration, including a large chunk of frieze from a Wright commission.

At the other side of the building was the library. This is one of Wright's most ingenious spaces, in which idealized geometry using multiple octagons, rectangles, and squares produces a satisfying space. The trim actually makes a potentially too-complicated scheme work, pulling together disparate shapes and imposing

The height of the second floor drum of the drafting room is lessened thanks to the stone-and-shingle barrier along the sidewalk.

human scale. It was perfect for its intended purpose, client meetings, where Wright could display the drawings and walk the homeowner-to-be through a proposed plan. The space had only a skylight and clerestory windows, meaning the client in the library, like the designers in the drafting room, would not be distracted from the business at hand by exterior views, yet there would be ample natural light during the day. The lack of visual contact with the world outside also provided the illusion of complete separation from the street which was, in fact, only a few feet away. The visitor was welcomed into the inner sanctum to be initiated into the mysteries of Wright's designs.

It may seem obvious that Frank Lloyd Wright was a gifted draftsman; yet his drafting skill cannot be separated from his architectural vision. While his colleague Marion Mahony may have prepared more artistic drawings than he did (during the Oak Park years, he used her drawings for presentations whenever he could), Wright the magician was nowhere more in evidence than when sitting at the drafting table. His particular brand of geometric legerdemain required triangles and a T-square. More than one memoir of working with Wright puts him at a drafting table, pencils meticulously sharpened, his hands moving with fluidity as buildings seemed to appear at a remarkable speed. Sometimes he drew so quickly he didn't even sit down; at others, he labored over drawings off and on for months, applying colors and even diffusing them with a razor blade, blending in graphite from other pencils, erasing and working the powders into a patina.

This skill may be, in part, a logical consequence of block play, of Wright's joyful massaging of Froebel's Gifts. As a preschooler, he learned to make buildings of blocks; later he was able to precipitate the essentials of an imagined structure on paper. His experiments with octagons imposed on squares; his fondness for squared-off moldings, fillets rather than astragals; his abstraction of irregular organic shapes into highly regular figures–all these habits bespeak the connection between his tools and his art. In looking at Wright's early work, rarely is one struck by its plastic, sculptural qualities. It is linear and rectilinear rather than curvaceous and voluptuous. While his tools can hardly be said to define his work, Wright rarely worked freehand and even the ornamental detailing he did for Sullivan in the early days, which relied upon botanical allusion such as leafy tendrils, was the product of drafting tools like French curves. As is so often true, his artistry emerged not by chance or in a moment's inspiration; creativity was more often born of highly disciplined work. Nowhere is this more in evident than in the library at the studio.

The Home and Studio today is a wonderful introduction to Wright. Even visitors unversed in architecture find themselves experiencing the transformation in the fledgling designer as he devised a new vocabulary. A contemporary of Wright's would have found the original house congenial, as it was essentially a vernacular, late Victorian home, albeit one with some intriguing variations. The entrance was obvious; inside, the first-floor plan was an open and transparent arrangement of public spaces. Within a decade, however, Wright had moved on, and his nascent prairie style was emerging.

Today, that sense of change is the secret of its appeal: the story line is that of an architectural evolution occurring before the visitor's eyes. It certainly isn't a successful overall design; it is more of a collision of styles. As architecture, it is an apprentice work grafted onto an early indication of the unprecedented work to come. Taken together, the Home and Studio is a rich collection of studies, of cartoons in the traditional sense of preparatory drawings, of ideas aborning. In short, the complex is a fully realized, three-dimensional sketchbook in which the artist can be seen growing and maturing.

The seeming opposition of the home and the studio was reflected by an emotional dichotomy in Wright himself. In his writings, he compared his professional regard for his work to his paternal feelings for his children. His thoughts were revealing. "Is it a quality?" he wrote. "Fatherhood? If so, I seemed born without it. And yet a building was a child. I have the father-feeling, I am sure, when coming back after a long time to one

The gable of the original home is almost lost from the Chicago Avenue elevation, just managing to peek over the deep overhanging roofs of the studio complex.

of my buildings. That must be the true feeling of fatherhood. But I never had it for my children. I had affection for them. I regarded them as with me—and play-fellows, comrades to be responsible for." His candid assessment of his patriarchal tendencies goes far to explain his behavior at the close of the Oak Park decades.

Wright defied the staid architectural tradition of Oak Park when he built his studio, but he invited the condemnation of his neighbors when, on an autumn day in 1909, he borrowed money from a client, using Japanese prints from his collection as collateral. That afternoon he caught a train for New York. Together with his lover, Martha Borthwick Cheney, he boarded a ship bound for Europe. He was not to return to the United States for a full year.

While circumstances might seem to suggest that his departure was impulsive, such decisions are rarely made in a day. His relationship with the woman familiarly known as Mamah Cheney (*MAY-ma CHEE-knee*) had begun much earlier, perhaps as a consequence of a friendship that developed, ironically, between Mamah and Catherine Wright. In 1903, Wright had designed an Oak Park home for Mamah and her husband, Edward, and he had frequently been observed squiring her around town. It is also clear that Wright had been unhappy in his marriage for some time.

The ostensible reason Wright gave the press at the time of his departure was his need to complete two volumes to be published by the German publisher Ernst Wasmuth. Ever concerned with close supervision of his work, Wright wished to be on hand to prepare the last of the drawings, many of which were the work of Marion Mahony, for the folio *Ausgeführte Bauten und Entwürfe von Frank Lloyd Wright* (which was to become familiarly known as the Wasmuth portfolio). The second, companion volume was a collection of photographs, titled *Frank Lloyd Wright Ausgeführte Bauten*. Wright himself was underwriting the cost of publication.

Once the visitor gets behind the wall, the impact of the studio and its grounds is to enclose and welcome.

When published in 1910 and 1911, respectively, the books had little American impact but did secure Wright's international renown, and they remain today key documents in the published canon of Frank Lloyd Wright. But it was the elopement with Mrs. Cheney that truly altered the course of his career. The scandal of his abandonment of his wife and children was reported on the front page of every Chicago paper. Not only did it effectively end his first marriage, but his adultery provoked outrage in staid Oak Park, a town where, as one Congregational minister put it, "the saloons stop and the steeples start." Upon his return, he found his services were no longer sought after and he was exiled from Oak Park, leading to the closure of what had been the most visible architectural practice there (even today, the thirty-odd Wright structures in Oak Park and neighboring River Forest remain the town's principal attraction to visitors).

Yet the termination of Wright's marriage and his two-decades-long association with Oak Park is better seen not as an end but as a dramatic *entr'acte*. In examining Wright's life as if it were a three-act drama played out in large measure in his three personal households, the departure from the Home and Studio signaled a new beginning in Spring Green, Wisconsin. There he would build (and continually rebuild) Taliesin, one of the most satisfying buildings of his long career. His life in Spring Green would also prove to be both a continual homecoming and a liberation, personally and professionally.

The Home and Studio today looks much as it did when Wright left in 1909, but that has not always been the case. When he embarked upon his new life at Taliesin, he sealed off the studio from the house with a brick firewall and redesigned both as independent domiciles. The home became a rental apartment while Wright converted the studio into a home for his family. Ironically, it was only after Wright left Catherine for another woman that his children, four of whom remained at home, got their own rooms in the converted space that had been the balcony of the studio.

The lower level of the drafting room became the living room, Wright's office the dining room, and the old passageway to the house a kitchen. He changed the mass of the drafting room's building, squaring off the octagonal shape to add living space for the upstairs bedrooms. Wright eventually sold the house in 1925, and other owners subsequently subdivided the structure again, at one time into seven distinct rental units. The last in a series of private owners put it up for sale in 1974, when the National Trust purchased it.

Between 1974 and 1987, a $2.2 million restoration turned the clock back. It involved not merely peeling back the later layers and restoring elements that had been removed in renovations, but also constructing new foundations. Wright's pattern in building his own dwellings was to build things inexpensively; at the Oak Park studio, as at Taliesin, uneven settlement had resulted, producing structural problems. The frame of the drafting room was also underbuilt, which meant that floor joists, rafters, and corner posts were all woefully undersized, leading to deflection even in Wright's own time. The playroom addition had been built with too-short collar ties, meaning the burden of the roof structure had caused the flanking walls to bend outward. The restoration had to undo many later changes to Wright's fabric, but it also had to correct structural shortcomings. (Wright often pushed the proverbial envelope, constructing structures that tested engineering limits; more than a few failures resulted, as the well-publicized problems at Fallingwater and his frequently leaky roofs suggest.)

Yet the Home and Studio rewards close study. Even the most resolute Wrightians admit it is far from a coherent masterpiece. Built by fits and starts, by a man who was usually short of money and forever changing his mind, the Home and Studio stands as a testament that the road of genius is a crooked one.

The house was anticipated by other structures built in the shingle style, most immediately those by Wright's first mentor, Silsbee. The studio, too, had as its

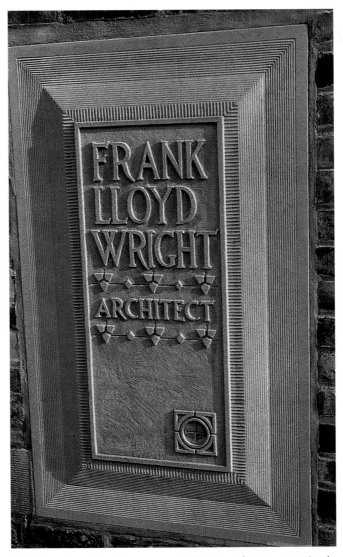

Wright's understated signage was little more than an oversized business card affixed to one side of the entrance porch.

antecedent most obviously the great mid-Victorian vogue for octagonal houses launched by Orson Squire Fowler (1809–1887). In his widely popular book *A Home for All* (1848), Fowler argued that the circle was nature's chosen building form but allowed that, given the inherent difficulty of building circular structures (traditional building materials are virtually all rectilinear), the octagon was next best since it was easier to construct yet shared the circle's advantage–namely that, in Fowler's opinion, it was a healthy and efficient form of building. It also produces maximum volume in a minimum of wall space, as well as maximum light and ventilation. Fowler's rationalization was the kind of eccentric philosophizing Wright himself would display over the years.

Yet Wright's studio was in no sense a derivative work. In fact, it was the springboard for much new and remarkable work; by the time of Wright's departure in 1909, he had completed some 125 buildings in his studio, among them most of his prairie style houses and several monumental public buildings, including the Larkin Administration Building in Buffalo, New York, and Unity Temple a few blocks away on Oak Park's Lake Street. The Home and Studio is a landmark in American architecture, notable as a point of origin, a creative place.

Still the Home and Studio should not be seen as the work of the Wright we usually think of, the *éminence grise* who speaks to us from documentary footage. The house was the work of a virtual boy, one still working in the shadow of his masters, groping to develop his own style and grammar. The studio was built by a man barely thirty, and both the house and the attached studio were built and rebuilt over a period of almost twenty years. The combined structure is neither prairie nor shingle style, though there are elements that anticipate the former and look back upon the latter. It was not born of a single epiphany; it was a testing ground, a crucible for experimentation, where Wright is thought to have rearranged rooms at least once a year.

Wright later dismissed his Oak Park house as "a youthful indiscretion." To anyone seeking to understand his work, however, the Home and Studio, as it evolved organically, is nothing less than an autobiographical icon of Wright's early development.

From the southwest, peaceful Taliesin hovering on its ridge, reflected in the calm waters of the pond below.

II TALIE/IN

/pring Green, Wisconsin

Wright returned to the Home and Studio after his European sojourn, but he would soon leave again, this time permanently. He planned to establish a new life with Mamah Cheney, now Mamah Borthwick after she reclaimed her maiden name. Upon his final departure in 1911, he traveled not to some foreign clime but to a place well known to him, one that exercised a compelling and complex lure.

Wright returned to Wisconsin to property owned by his mother whose doting support was an important resource for him until her death in 1923. The farmland in the Helena Valley was more than a safe harbor from the storm of controversy he left behind. It was the ancestral landscape on which his maternal grandparents,

Wright provided visitors to Taliesin with a convenient vantage from which to view Taliesin, a small island in the man-made pond reached by crossing a simple wooden bridge.

Richard and Mary Lloyd Jones, had homesteaded. Termed the "driftless area" by geologists, the terrain in the Helena Valley was unusual because it had been protected by hills to the north from the scrape-and-fill action of the glacier during the Pleistocene epoch. Having immigrated from Wales, the Lloyd Joneses had immediately felt at home in the lush landscape. As a youngster Wright, too, had found there the closest thing he had known to a permanent home. It had become a haven from the peripatetic existence that was the result of his father's frequent job changes.

Another important attraction of the Helena Valley was that it was rural. Wright's organic philosophy was taking shape and he had come to understand that his creative energies were stimulated less by the built environment than by changing seasons, day-to-day weather events, and the cycle of the sun. His dream for his Wisconsin home, to be located in a community of farmers, was essentially agrarian. Over a period of forty-eight years, from his return in 1911 to his death in 1959, Taliesin would grow to become not only his home and studio but also a laboratory for his ideas. It would be the site of his communal experiment in teaching and practicing architecture, as well as a place of tragedy.

Wright's brazen behavior in the previous years had established him as newsworthy, so any dispatch concerning him was sure to catch the eye of reporters. Initial Chicago press accounts in mid 1911 about his Wisconsin project reported that ground had been broken for a Wright house–that much was true–but that it was to be a cottage for Anna Lloyd Wright. By Christmas of that year Wright had moved into the nearly completed house and was ready to set the record straight. He called a press conference and announced that the house was to be for him and Martha Borthwick. He told the assembled reporters that the place was to be called Taliesin.

Thanks to Wright, the name Taliesin (pronounced *talley-ESS-in*) has a place in architecture's iconography, but it didn't begin as a builder's word. Taliesin was a Druid bard-prophet who extolled the beauty of art at the court of Camelot. He was also notable for his appearance, in particular his radiant brow. Wright the lover of language adopted the name, which means "shining brow" in Welsh. Both its mythological and its Welsh origins appealed to Wright but, more to the point, it nicely described the siting of his new house.

As a boy Wright had on occasion escaped the toil of farm labor to a hilltop where he daydreamed, enjoying a lofty view of the surrounding countryside. In his *Autobiography*, he recalled finding there a harbinger of spring, the pasque flower (*Anemone patens*), pushing through the snow. The pasque flower is a characteristic grassland species and is thus a poetically appropriate antecedent to Taliesin, perhaps Wright's finest prairie house.

"It was unthinkable to me," Wright wrote, "that any house should be put on that beloved hill. I knew well that no house should ever be on a hill or on anything. It should be of the hill." The on-versus-of opposition became a keynote to Wright's thinking about organic architecture. While he was known to violate the "not-on" tenet when he saw fit, at Taliesin, true to the name he gave it, the house does not sit at the top of the

hill; the knob is still a grassy bump amid the sprawl of the enormous building. Taliesin is literally a shining brow, the house very much a part of its headland overlooking the lake and the rolling contours of the farmlands that surround it.

In designing the house, Wright was influenced by his time in Europe, much of which he spent near Florence, in Fiesole. If Taliesin is one of Wright's most memorable accomplishments–and in the opinion of many, it is–it is something more as well. It is the product of a refreshed imagination. Wright had escaped a marriage and the repetitions of his increasingly stolid practice in Oak Park, and had gone to Italy. When he returned, he settled in his Wisconsin valley, which he described as being very like Tuscany. He proceeded to build a home that, from a distance, bears a considerable resemblance to a Tuscan villa with its tile roof and earth-brown stucco walls planted on a hillside.

Taliesin provided Wright with a dual opportunity to exercise his skill with buildings and his penchant for the rhetorical flourish. Wright sought to build a "natural house." His conception of the house included fruit trees and berry bushes, strawberries and asparagus, and a herd of Holsteins, along with horses and even peacocks. From the start, he envisioned Taliesin as a great deal more than the Home and Studio had been. In addition to being a permanent domicile for Wright and Martha Borthwick (and a sometime home for her children),

Raised on its limestone piers, the southeast and main façade of Taliesin looks haughty and forbidding.

From the top of the hill north of Taliesin, the manifold hipped roofs still reflect the surrounding topography although in the reconstruction that was Taliesin III, some were raised, making the overall structure less submissive to the surrounding terrain.

there was to be a drafting room and office space for his architectural practice, which from the start would include apprentices. To the rear of the complex would be a cottage for farm laborers and draftsmen, as well as garages and even farm buildings. Taliesin, Wright wrote, "was to be a complete living unit, genuine in point and comfort and beauty, from pig to proprietor."

Taliesin today is true to Wright's original conception. Yet this is a house that has had more incarnations than Thomas Jefferson's Monticello. Jefferson, greatly admired by Wright, observed that "Architecture is my delight and putting up, and pulling down, one of my favorite amusements." He

Above the seated Japanese figure and the art pottery vase, the diagonal lines of ceiling help define the space. Those lines are applied strips of lath, perhaps the cheapest wood product available, which Wright used in a fashion that emulated Japanese design. As extravagant as he could be with his clients' money, at times he could also make a lot with a little.

Under Wright's watchful eye, the quarried stone was laid up horizontally, with rough surfaces facing out. The look was strongly horizontal, but from one course to the next the stones corbeled in or out to enho the effect of natural strata.

A third side of the inner courtyard is enclosed to the southwest by the so-called Hill Wing of the house (it is near the acme of the hill). The fourth side of the inner garden—the vantage from which this photograph was taken—is open to the south and the rolling hills that are the site of Tan-Y-Deri, the Midway Farm, and the Hillside School.

The studio wing on the left and the main living area of the house on the right embrace a sunken courtyard. It a self-contained microcosm of plantscape and hardscape that contrasts to the broad vistas on the other side of the house.

The doorway isn't immediately apparent as the visitor approaches the stairs. The entrance wasn't always here on the northeast elevation as early visitors to Taliesin drove a loop that virtually encircled the house and arrived on the opposite side of the home.

and Wright both spent nearly a half-century each at their principal homes doing a great deal of putting up and pulling down. In Wright's case, it was not solely the result of rethinking design decisions, though there was an untold number of renovations born of fresh ideas. There were also two major fires at Taliesin.

On August 14, 1914, a servant in an insane rage set fire to the house. He ignited gasoline in the living quarters and, in less than an hour, the main wing was a smoking ruin. Wright had been in Chicago supervising the last details of his Midway Gardens project. When he got word of the fire, he quickly boarded a train for Spring Green. Along the way, he learned the full extent of the tragedy. The arsonist had attacked and killed Mamah Borthwick, her two children, and four others with a hatchet. He then swallowed a quantity of hydrochloric acid and, though he lived on for several weeks in a nearby jail, he was unable to eat or speak and took with him to his grave his rationale for his actions.

Mamah's remains were interred within sight of Taliesin in the Unity Chapel burial ground. She was the great love of Wright's life, and his remains would eventually be buried beside hers (though not for long, as the magisterial Olgivanna, Wright's third wife, had them moved to Arizona to be at her grave site). While he suffered "a kind of black despair," Wright found relief, a sort of mournful therapy, in setting about to construct Taliesin II, its first incarnation having been dubbed Taliesin I (1911-1914).

A jog at one end of the living room leads to small dining area and a doorway that, in turn, gives access to the bird walk. A walk to its end, some forty feet out from the mass of the building, is to be rewarded by the sensation of being suspended in space while surrounded by Wright's valley to the southeast

Taliesin II was as ill-fated as its predecessor. Wright was more often absent than in residence between 1916 and 1922, when he spent extended periods in Japan at work on the Imperial Hotel and then in California as he attempted to build his practice there, constructing among other projects four of his "textile-block" houses. Despite his frequent absences, his Wisconsin home became a repository for his rapidly growing collection of Japanese artifacts. Walls were adorned with screens and the house was dotted with sculpture, block prints, and embroidered fabrics on pillows and tables.

In the living room, the areas meld into one another. The dining space (center) features Wright's barrel chairs and a Japanese screen painting. The fireplace is to the right, the ribbon of southeast facing windows that backs the seating area to the left.

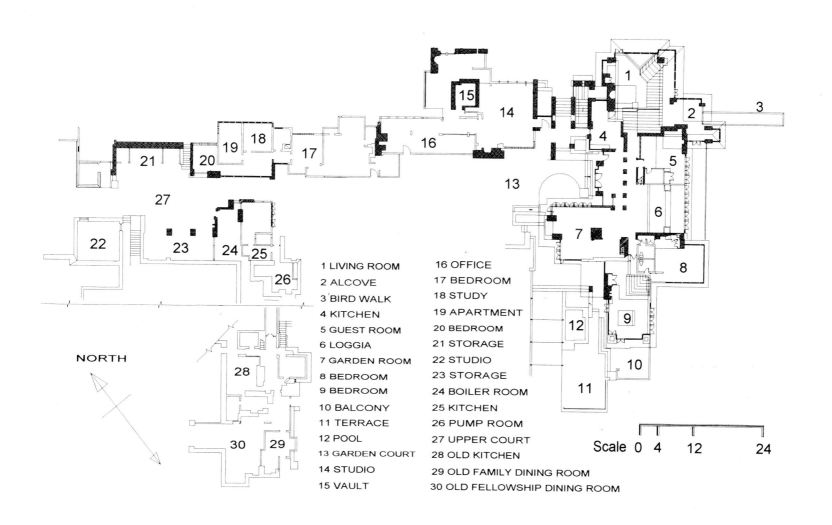

1 LIVING ROOM
2 ALCOVE
3 BIRD WALK
4 KITCHEN
5 GUEST ROOM
6 LOGGIA
7 GARDEN ROOM
8 BEDROOM
9 BEDROOM
10 BALCONY
11 TERRACE
12 POOL
13 GARDEN COURT
14 STUDIO
15 VAULT

16 OFFICE
17 BEDROOM
18 STUDY
19 APARTMENT
20 BEDROOM
21 STORAGE
22 STUDIO
23 STORAGE
24 BOILER ROOM
25 KITCHEN
26 PUMP ROOM
27 UPPER COURT
28 OLD KITCHEN
29 OLD FAMILY DINING ROOM
30 OLD FELLOWSHIP DINING ROOM

NORTH

Scale 0 4 12 24

The floorplan of Taliesin III

Then the second incarnation of Taliesin burned, this time as a result of faulty wiring. The 1925 conflagration again burned most of the living space of the house. Wright himself detected the fire when he observed smoke spewing from his bedroom windows. He helped fight the flames, but it was a violent thunderstorm and the attendant downpour that finally doused the fire. The damage was estimated between one-quarter and half a million dollars, but Wright, despite the fact that his professional career was at a low, knew immediately what he wanted to do. He later wrote, "I went to work again to build better than before because I had learned from building the other two."

That fire typified Wright's life in the mid-1920s. The financial burden of rebuilding Taliesin forced him to sell the Home and Studio, long a rental property, for $33,500. Business at his practice was slow, with fewer commissions in the works than at any other time in his career. He remarried in 1923, this time to Miriam Noel, a self-consciously artistic socialite with whom Wright became infatuated in the months after the 1914 fire. Though they had been together almost a decade, the marriage lasted barely five months. A bitter legal battle ensued, culminating in Wright's temporarily losing title to Taliesin. Only the intervention of a band of his friends and clients, who purchased shares in a venture called Wright, Inc., succeeded in returning him to his residence.

Called the "Blue Loggia," this room is a transition space from the living room on one end of the house to Wright's private quarters on the other. While Wright favored red and taupe, blue was Olgivanna's color.

Wright captured the majestic southerly view through his bold band of windows. No conversation in this living room was without a natural backdrop.

The studio is reached by moving back through the entrance to the first wing to the rear. A string of north windows help light the drafting tables while the mass of the fire-proof vault of stone for Wright's treasures (both his drawings and Japanese prints) is on the left.

Just as Wright's life seemed at its most discombobulated, it regained some equilibrium. The stabilizing influence came in the unlikely form of a European-born divorcée thirty years his junior. He met Olga Ivanovna Milanoff Hinzenberg at a matinee performance in Chicago of the Petrograd Ballet. According to Wright, that very afternoon he fell in love.

Olgivanna, as she was familiarly known, was young and lithe, but perhaps equally important was her air of mystery. She had been born in Montenegro, then a mountainous kingdom on the Balkan peninsula, later a constituent republic of Yugoslavia. The daughter of a prominent judge and the granddaughter of a general, she had been educated in Russia and Turkey. Married as a teenager to a Russian architect named Vlademar Hinzenberg, she bore him a daughter, Svetlana, before leaving her husband and moving to Paris.

In France she enrolled in Georgi Gurdjieff's Institute for the Harmonious Development of Man. She became a teacher of movement, a discipline key to Gurdjieff's philosophy. He believed that the modern world had robbed mankind of its essential balance, and that only by hard work, contemplation, and self-exploration could that harmony be restored. Olgivanna was among the disciples who traveled to the United States with Gurdjieff for a dance exhibition at Carnegie Hall, and she had gone on to Chicago to meet with Hinzenberg to resolve matters concerning the end of their marriage. It proved a fateful detour as she met Wright, and within months of their chance meeting they were ensconced at Taliesin. In December of 1925, she gave birth to Wright's last child, daughter Iovanna (though he would later adopt Svetlana). Olgivanna would be with him until his death, and for a

quarter-century afterward, she would be the zealous guardian of his fame, as president of the Frank Lloyd Wright Foundation (established in 1940).

Their home, Taliesin III (1925-59 and after), is the building that stands today.

If the Home and Studio was self-contained, a house that seemed to avert its eyes from the streets, Taliesin looks boldly out to its environs. In part this is because it is a country manor dominating the valley that is its demesne, a vista very different from the increasingly dense streetscape of Oak Park that Wright had left behind. Like a castle, Taliesin from its hill commands the respect of those who approach, the lake before it a virtual moat reflecting and protecting the stone-and-stucco stronghold. Wright, having faced the censure of his neighbors in Oak Park, built himself a protective refuge.

Yet Taliesin is no forbidding fortress. This castle isn't dominated by a tower. On the contrary, like the wings of an unimaginably large eagle, its low roofs seem to shadow the brow of the hill. In planning Taliesin, Wright consciously mimicked the lines of the surrounding hills. The house is very much of its context, the

hipped roofs echoing the horizon line, the pitches duplicating the slopes of nearby ridges and crests.

Stone for the house was quarried from another hill a mile away. Teams of horses driven by local farmers hauled the stone to the building site, where it became the foundation for the building. It was laid up as terraces, low walls, and tall masonry chimney masses that featured, on the interior of the home, great stone hearths with cavernous fireboxes. Fireplaces were fundamental to the Wright code, but it was at Taliesin that he first abandoned brick for stone in building them. Wright directed that the stone be laid in a way that resembled the stratified layers in the sedimentary bed where it had formed, so the house might appear to be founded on a natural outcropping of the sand-colored limestone.

Above the stone work, a wood-framed structure was built (and rebuilt), its exterior surface parged with stucco, its color the gray of Portland cement. Inside, the plaster was golden, thanks to pigments added to the mix.

If this was a manor house–and in some ways it was–then in a sense it was also an owner-built home with the mix of amateur implications that the term suggests. Of course Wright didn't build it alone. Taliesin I and II were built by local builders, workmen of Irish, Norwegian, and Italian extraction. Some of them worked for Wright for a dozen years and more. But much of the fabric of Taliesin III has the charm of the handmade, assembled by inexperienced apprentices, students of Wright's who were learning by doing. Unlike the fine craftsmanship he specified for his well-to-do clients–art-glass windows, specially commissioned sculptural elements, sophisticated millwork and metalwork, and more–Taliesin was the work of a mix of willing amateurs and an occasional professional, all working with ordinary materials. The basic ingredients are little more than local stone, cypress trim, and plaster.

A descendent of the Inglenook, this fireplace on the north wall of the living room also represents Wright's own take on the fireplace, with a giant limestone lintel and stylized crane. Every major room at Taliesin has a fireplace and, while no two are the same, they share a style of masonry that is calculatedly casual.

Two of Wright's barrel chairs, masterpieces of machine-made geometry, before the craggy silhouettes of a forest backdrop, produce a surprisingly harmonious mix.

The floor plans for many of Wright's prairie style houses had an obvious geometric logic. He used T-, L-, and cruciform-shaped plans. Some of those houses were linear, others boxy, but each had a regularity, even a symmetry, about its overall conception. In contrast, Taliesin's five-wing composition was dictated by no axis, grid, or other evident organizing principle.

The largest wing contained the living quarters with the main façade overlooking the pond. Extending northeast was the studio wing which connected with the hill wing to the southwest to embrace the inner courtyard, which featured the "tea circle," an assemblage of stone blocks at the foot of a large oak. At the hub of Taliesin, the tea circle was the place where work was often interrupted by impromptu gatherings and where Wright held court. Behind the hill wing were two parallel wings to the northwest. Like a New England farm house that evolved to suit its owners' needs, Taliesin is a unique big house with numerous little houses, back houses, and barns snaking over the hill. The wings are of various heights, ranging from one to three stories.

In Wright's time, Taliesin grew to be an enormous complex, as the interior of the house—including Wright's quarters, the living and dining areas, guest rooms, garages, animal sheds, and the rest—is just shy of an acre at 37,000 square feet.

To enter Taliesin, as is usual with the mature Wright's style, is to encounter misdirection. In more traditional architecture, the front door is the proverbial nose on the house's face, obvious, easy to find. At Taliesin, finding the door requires guesswork (there are multiple turns and sets of steps outside). Having found the door, one must follow a meandering path through a low entry hall to the first living space. Wright's trademark use of varying ceiling heights is in evidence, setting up the visitor for the soaring ceiling to come.

The living room has been described more than once as the best American domestic space, yet such superlatives don't capture its uniqueness. To borrow Noel Coward's title, it is a "design for living." This isn't a look-at-me space; its materials are modest in the extreme. In fact, the same materials are used on the inside of Taliesin as on the outside—limestone on floors and fireplaces, plaster on the walls. These materials also serve to blur the lines between exterior and interior.

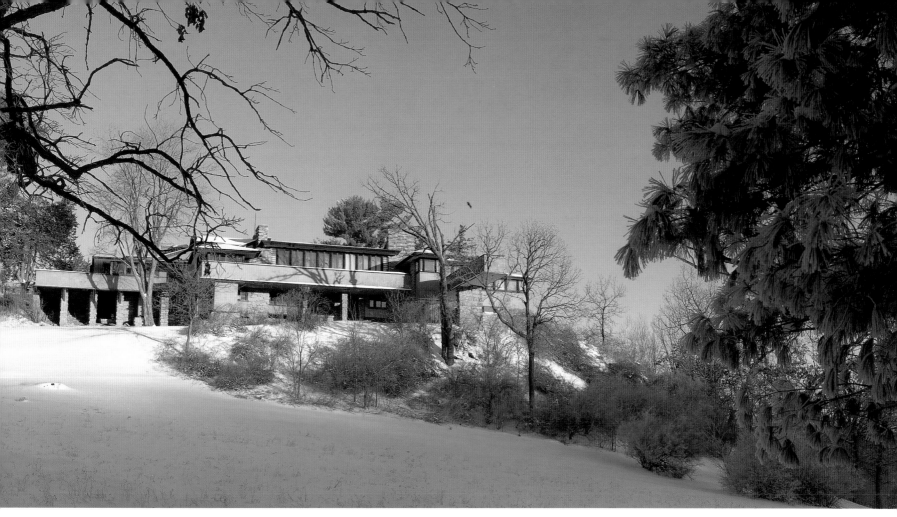

In his *Autobiography*, Wright wrote of Taliesin, "[It's] a house of the north. The whole was low, wide and snug, a broad shelter seeking fellowship in its surroundings."

Wright's enchanment with things oriental is frequently in evidence, as in this view of a Buddha gazing at a Japanese screen.

There are unmistakable Wright touches on the stage at the Taliesin Theater, in particular his four-sided music stand and the curtain, a geometric design that is actually an abstraction of the Helena Valley, with its fields, hills, and barns.

Amid its lush landscape, Taliesin has a noble view of Mr. Wright's realm.

This is a complex room, one to which a great deal of dense analytical prose has been devoted. It is a large, unified space, yet, as Wright would later do so well with the modest common rooms in his Usonian homes, he created distinct areas without actual room divisions. Within the twenty-eight by thirty-six foot space, the fireplace is one focus, the dining area another. There is also a large seating area and access to a unique terrace, the bird walk.

The ceiling soars above. A line of windows draws the eye to unspoiled acres outside. The room contains many pieces of what is perhaps the largest collection of Wright-designed furniture, much of it designed specifically for Taliesin. Some is for sitting, but many pieces are built-in shelves and display niches that contain Buddhist figures, Chinese pottery, carpets, and trays. Notably, the objects are not insulated from the life of the house by glass cases or velvet ropes. The art is of the living space, just as the house is of the hill.

Throughout the house, Japanese Momoyama screens are key elements in certain tableau. Wright started collecting Japanese prints in 1905 on his first visit there; he was both a passionate collector and an occasional dealer (though he seemed reluctant to part with them; most of the sales seem to have occurred when his periodic financial distress was most acute). Taliesin has much Japanese art, ranging from prints to sculptural objects. Some is of museum quality, some little more than tourist junk. But all achieve the decorative effect that Wright wanted.

Wright's bedroom is at the extreme opposite end of the main house. In this room, he gave in to his penchant to play with ceiling heights, reaching a new low as in some areas the clearance is barely six feet. In contrast, the room has a panoramic view to the south. Stepping outside to its balcony is to be reminded again of Taliesin's connection to its place. The vantage is of Unity Chapel and most of the other buildings on the property, dependencies almost as essential to the estate as the house itself. During the decades when Wright was in residence, he expanded his holdings to some 3,000 acres. Along with the fields and pastures, he acquired a num-

Wright's work is almost always more comprehensible than his words:
Taliesin is indeed a house that seems to have emerged from its site.

Wright was seeking in his organic architecture an elemental connectedness to nature. Trees were a recurring symbol for him and
just outside the foyer to the theater at Hillside, the roof and a
tremendous tree actually intersect, with the tissues of the tree
swallowing more and more of the overhang over the decades.

ber of structures, several of which he designed, including the Romeo and Juliet Windmill (1896), the Hillside Home School (1903), the dwelling Tan-Y-Deri (1907), and the Midway Farm (1938).

From his bedroom, Wright also had a view of the pond. Upon his return to Wisconsin in 1911, a spring-fed stream ran through the Valley of the God-Almighty Jones (a nickname coined by neighbors in recognition of the fact that the Lloyd Joneses were lords of their own valley and that also suggests something of the Lloyd Joneses' high assessment of themselves; Wright came by his hauteur honestly). Almost immediately, Wright ordered that a stone dam be constructed. This had a practical purpose, as the water held back by the dam flooded nearby low-lying acreage to form a pond. Water could then be pumped to the top of the hill, where it cycled through the fountains and watered the gardens. The lake itself also became part of the viewscape from Taliesin. Wright admired nature and extolled its virtues; when it suited him, however, he didn't hesitate to change it.

The same calculated management of nature is in evidence in the immediate environs of the house. There are manicured flower gardens that set off the hardscape of stone walls and terraces, as well as paths and outdoor sculpture that accentuate features in the landscape. The balconies and planters soften the transition from

This may be Wright's earliest building (how much of the 1896 design is to be atributed to J. Lyman Silisbee is subject to debate), but without doubt the Unity Chapel had rich emotional and familial connections for Wright throughout his life.

Like the future Taliesin, the principle building materials at the Hillside Home School were local stone, wood, and stucco. In this picture, the cubic volume on the left dates from the original 1902 design, but is linked to the 1932 drafting studio by a forty-foot timber bridge.

indoor to outdoor spaces, while bushes and trees provide a buffer to the farm acreage. The net effect is to integrate the house into its setting. As Wright wrote, "The house began to associate with the ground, and became natural to its prairie site."

In 1902, Wright designed the HILLSIDE HOME SCHOOL for his aunts, Ellen (Nell) and Jane Lloyd Jones. It was built the following year on what had been the original farmstead, established by Wright's maternal grandparents, Richard and Mary Lloyd Jones, who bequeathed the property to the unmarried sisters. An earlier school dating from 1887 and Wright's first solo design effort had occupied some of the same site but was later completely demolished. It is survived only by a few photographic images that portray its gabled and shingled Victorian facade.

For the new school, his aunts presented Wright with a program that neatly coincided with his own emerging notions of organic architecture. The school had already been in business for fifteen years. Its first enrollees consisted largely of nieces and nephews, but the school gradually acquired a national reputation. The educational philosophy was to integrate the natural world with that of the classroom. Nature study, hikes through the surrounding acres, outdoor classes, and picnics were part of its progressive approach. Wright clearly approved, as he sent his two eldest sons, Lloyd and John, to study there.

This was Wright's route on foot or behind the wheel of one of his cars from his home to the studio at the Hillside Home School.

Wright's oft-used barb, "inferior desecrators," characterizes how he felt about interior decorators. Nevertheless he had his own ideas about interior design, which favored Japanese screens, rectilinear furniture of his own design, and always flowers, fresh or dried.

The Hillside School anticipated a number of innovations that Wright would later use in other institutional structures. Superficially, the seesaw design of two large boxes linked by an axis resembled his own Oak Park studio, as well as the much-admired Unity Temple in Oak Park (1904). Thematically, the exterior expression of the masses of the primary interior volumes anticipated such works as the Larkin Administration Building (1903). At Hillside, the major masses originally enclosed a gymnasium and an assembly hall, while the connective structure contained classrooms and a gallery/hallway. Wright built his aunts a structure that seemed to rise out of the ground, paralleling the horizon. In fact, the Hillside School is one of Wright's earliest prairie buildings (though not a residential building, it nevertheless resembles a prairie house).

The program for the Hillside School, both as conceived and as it evolved, anticipated Wright's own Taliesin Fellowship, and not only in function. Both were schools and both took an intimate, almost familial approach to the education process. The building as its stands today reflects the latter institutional use, as the aunts closed their school in 1915 and, at their deaths, willed the property to Wright. In 1932, Wright used the derelict building to help launch the Taliesin Fellowship.

He converted the gym into a dramatic theater (the Hillside Playhouse) which, after a fire in 1952, was again remodeled. The classrooms became a dining room. In the 1932 renovation, a 5,000-square-foot drafting studio was added to the north, reached via a "bridge" linking it to the main east-west axis of the original building. Today, the building encloses galleries, a dining room, kitchen, student rooms, and a common room with a colossal fireplace.

The Taliesin Fellowship proved to be a visionary mix of architectural firm, commune, design school, farm, and hero worship, all centered upon Mr. Wright. The "School for the Allied Arts," as he had initially described it in 1931, saw the first apprentices arrive to enroll in what came to be known familiarly as the Taliesin Fellowship. Wright had long had apprentices at hand, but the larger and more formal Fellowship proved an

invigorating change in Wright's life. He turned sixty-five that year and many had written him off as a rather peculiar and garrulous old man who hadn't built a significant building in a decade or more. But the partnership that was his marriage to Olgivanna was about to power Wright to new and remarkable achievements.

For a fee of $650 each, students were invited to join the educational experiment. Wright had done his best early work in the collegial and, to a degree, collaborative environs of his Oak Park studio. His had always been the dominant presence, but he had drawn energy from and utilized the ideas and skills of a number of his colleagues on the payroll at the studio. The Hillside Home School, along with the Oak Park studio and Gurdjieff's Institute for the Harmonious Development of Man, were among the Fellowship's progenitors.

The Taliesin Fellowship was as much a creation of Olgivanna as it was of Wright. This was no traditional architecture school, as music, dance, and even spiritualism were key elements in the training of apprentices. The Fellowship also aimed to be self-sufficient, requiring apprentices to work in the fields, barns, kitchen, or laundry.

Still, architecture dominated, beginning with the task of adapting the abandoned school to its new purposes. As Wright's practice burgeoned, senior apprentices made it possible for him to complete many more commissions than would have been practical for a small office. A number of apprentices executed drawings, not a few of which Wright himself signed. Apprentices often were assigned to job sites to function as clerks of the

Even in its derelict condition, there is a grandeur about the stone piers and foundation walls of a demolished shed, seeming to guard the surviving barns behind.

In any season, Taliesin seems suited to its setting, even with snow blurring the definition of its multiple roof planes.

works, Wright's eyes and ears supervising construction and reporting back on progress. This was hardly a community of equals, however: Not only was Mr. Wright the unchallenged "Master" (as he was sometimes known), but not all the apprentices were on the same plane. A senior core evolved that included Eugene Masselink, Wright's secretary; John Howe, who helped manage the drafting office; and William Wesley Peters, who was to marry Olgivanna's older daughter. Each of these men spent virtually their entire working lives toiling for Mr. and Mrs. Wright and the collective experiment that Taliesin became. The Fellowship was Wright's personal fiefdom: Apprenticeship, he said, is "much like it was in feudal times . . . an apprentice then was his master's slave; at Taliesin he is his master's comrade." Wright may have added an element of collegiality to the proceedings, but clearly he liked the feeling of being surrounded by courtiers. The Fellowship also served an important public relations function, bringing such talented youth as Edgar Kaufman Jr. into Wright's sphere. After a year's stay at Taliesin, Kaufman returned home and convinced his father that Wright was the man to design the family's weekend retreat in Bear Run, Pennsylvania. Fallingwater was the result.

Despite Wright's death in 1959, the Fellowship has survived as the Frank Lloyd Wright School of Architecture. Without Wright, though, its nature has changed. The apprenticeship approach had to be abandoned, superseded by a formal curriculum of courses that also enabled the school to receive accreditation as a school of architecture, a status it never had in Wright's lifetime. The curriculum became more traditional, its instructors drawn largely from the ranks of Taliesin Associated Architects (TAA), the architectural practice that inherited Wright's mantle. The merits of the school and the caliber of the work produced by TAA continues to be the subject of debate. But that the Fellowship invigorated Wright in his lifetime is beyond dispute.

Wright dubbed his house Taliesin, but the name came to refer to his larger estate, as the more extensive holdings he acquired over a period of decades began to resemble those of a true Italian villa. Today the term villa is often used to describe a country house, an escape from the city to the bucolic quiet of the countryside. But in Renaissance Italy, a villa was a country estate consisting of farmland, barns (or *barchesse*), gardens, vineyards, and a fortification or *castello* as well as a house. A villa was a pleasure palace but also a place of business. Thus, Taliesin can be seen as a twentieth-century variation on an old theme.

For purposes of typology, Wright might well have accepted such a description. Stylistically, however, he would have objected vociferously. He made many remarks over the decades to the effect that all was rotten with the state of architecture until he came along. He rejected the ritual adaptation of older forms from ancient Greece and Rome, such as the temple fronts and the orders so characteristic of the Renaissance villas of Palladio and others. In Wright's opinion, such historicist recycling failed to obey what he called "natural law" but, instead, relied upon what he regarded as the tired formulas of classical antiquity. He characterized such buildings

as "inorganic." The traditional notion of the villa, with its essential connectedness to the land, provides a complementary contrast to Wright's Taliesin, which is perhaps the perfect place to talk about "organic architecture." To understand Wright, understanding what he meant by organic architecture is essential.

Wright's childhood with his nuclear family was spent living in towns or small cities until circumstances drew the family back within the influence of his mother's family, the Lloyd Joneses. During his temporary but repeated habitations on his uncles' farms, he connected with the agrarian life and its rituals. The experience of his summer visits and his enduring affection for the

Moments of verticality for Wright at his homes were few, but at Taliesin he made the most of this one. The commission from his aunts for a windmill produced a memorable and unmistakably Wrightian statement.

Originally the bird walk reached into a copse of tall trees, giving it the feel of an aerie. Even bare of cover, the bird walk is a fitting place to admire Wright the chance-taker as it reaches into space.

Helena Valley lie at the foundation of his organic architecture. To look at the main house at Taliesin, as well as the Midway Farm buildings and the Hillside Home School, is to apprehend in three dimensions his philosophy.

Yet it must also be said that Wright's mentor, Louis Sullivan, probably introduced Wright to the notion of the organic. In Sullivan's prose, which was typically even more opaque than Wright's, "organic" was a favorite word. He anticipated Wright in regarding the architect as virtually a force of nature; Wright went further and made the architect a societal force as well. The organic for Sullivan was best symbolized by his biomorphic decorations, the dense detailing with intertwined leaves and vines. For Wright the organic implied an openness to the natural world, not solely in its details but to the landscape as a whole. For him, a good building was a metaphor for nature itself.

Wright talked often of organic architecture. He was highly articulate and had a dramatic presence, making him a captivating companion and a persuasive speaker. But his words tended to be more exhortative than

On the knob before the Tan-Y-Deri, a circle of chairs overlook the pastoral countryside, with a tractor at work in the middle distance and Taliesin at the horizon line.

precise. In reading Wright's prose, one is reminded that his father, both grandfathers, and an uncle were preachers.

Wright's organic philosophy is actually simpler than it sounds, and it is not as convoluted as his long string of "organic" utterances makes it seem. But straightforward assertions of what constitutes organic architecture invariably bring with them a range of broader implications and beg a number of questions. In general, much architectural criticism has a tendency to get rather hazy: the further one gets from first principles, the more subjective the verbiage becomes. When Wright spoke, his listeners often found themselves enchanted. It is easy to lose one's way in his imaginative thicket of forms and words. The illusion of simplicity is the first spell, followed by incantations of growing complexity. Wright talked specifically of the "spell power" of geometry. Certain shapes had meaning for him: the square represented integrity and the triangle stood for structural unity (as we will see in the next chapter, Taliesin West was laid out on a triangular plan). The circle meant unity and the spiral represented organic process; in his last decade, he became rather preoccupied with both the circle and the spiral.

In a basic definition of the organic, a key element is setting, the site and siting of a structure. According to Wright, the building must be integral with its environment. "My prescription for a modern house?" wrote Wright. "One–a good site. . . . [S]tanding on that site, look about so that you see what has charm. . . . Then build your house so that you may still look from where you stood upon all that charmed you and lose nothing of what you saw before the house was built. See that architectural association accentuates character." His notion is epitomized by Taliesin's low, hipped roof lines that so cleverly correspond to the contours of the surrounding terrain.

Setting is essential but hardly everything to organic architecture. The organic house was to grow from its site, but a corollary was that Wright believed buildings grew from the inside out: "Both plan and construction are to be inspired from within." Traditionally, architecture had been conceived from the outside in. Think of classical temples and even the simplest of gable-roofed houses. Each started with a mass (or masses) that

reflected a given set of traditions, tastes, and building materials. The volumes within evolved over time, but typically they were subsidiary to the overall conception of the exterior which established rhythms, symmetries, and patterns that predetermined much of the interior. Wright's organic architecture demanded a fundamental shift in the balance—the design should look outward.

This reversal of thinking proved widely popular, more so by far than any of Wright's stylistic innovations. Unfortunately, much of the bad architecture of the twentieth century reflects inside-out thinking, because most designers and builders lack Wright's skill at resolving the challenges it poses. Wright can hardly be blamed for the bad work of others; yet, in a sense, his widely varied pronouncements about organic architecture made it all too easy for people to adopt the elements of the organic they liked while ignoring others. In fact, he hadn't intended to shift the balance at all, but rather to integrate the outside into the interiors.

In practice, Wright himself used details to convey a sense of the organic in his buildings: "Each material speaks a language of its own." He didn't believe in painting wood but favored natural wood finishes that emphasized grain and texture. He decried the elaborately milled moldings and lathe-turned components that distinguished many Victorian styles. He favored colors in earth tones, browns and greens and especially

The name Tan-Y-Deri comes from the Welsh, meaning "under the oaks." And indeed it is nestled nicely into its setting, the horizontal board-and-batten siding seeming to lower its boxy profile.

"Cherokee red," the ferrous orangy-red he used repeatedly. He had a special fondness for stone and instructed that it be worked in a way that bespoke the patina of Mother Nature's wear and tear rather than the polish of man or machine.

Wright's organic philosophy began with buildings and the way in which they were to relate to their environment. His more encompassing view, however, concerned "the relationship of man to the cosmos." Two of his favorite words, "unity" and "nature," were the building blocks of his philosophy. To reduce his philosophy (as he never chose to do), "organic architecture" reflected a thoughtful "unity" of man and "nature." He sought, in constructing his buildings, including residential, civic, and ecclesiastical structures, to establish in them an organic unity of site, use, and even society. With mixed success, he attempted to design affordable buildings, to improve homes for average people. These were bold goals that have inspired many people and that he, more than once, managed to achieve.

Let's set aside the broader philosophy and seek to define organic *architecture*. Again, there is no single sentence in Wright's own words that satisfactorily summarizes it, but his various musings on the subject in *The Japanese Print*, *The Natural House*, his *Autobiography*, and other writings can be stripped to certain essentials.

In creating organic architecture, Wright sought to reconsider the nature of residential architecture, reducing it to fundamentals, then to translate those into native forms using indigenous materials that suited the culture, era, and location. Stated a simpler way, Wright proposed that houses suit the needs of their inhabitants and reflect their environments without regard to historical-cum-architectural precedent. However, as comprehensible and comprehensive as that may seem, Wright was always at hand to muddy the works: he acknowledged, as well, that no organic building is ever "finished."

Wright's organic philosophy is nothing if not another of his imaginative, paradoxical, and thought-provoking constructions. It isn't to be read or applied literally. For Wright, it was a kind of oral epic, one that varied from one recitation to the next. Wright might have been charmed by architectural historian Neil Levine's

poetic description of Taliesin. "Taliesin," he wrote, "is an incident in the landscape." A more cogent description of organic architecture would be difficult to find.

In the commission for a simple windmill, Wright saw an opportunity for a flight of fancy. In 1896, his maiden aunts, Nell and Jane Lloyd Jones, asked him to design for them a windmill. It was to pump water from an artesian well into a reservoir dug out of the rock atop the hill that rose behind their Hillside Home School. While a more utilitarian structure would have met their needs–their goal was simply to ensure that the school had a reliable supply of water–Wright produced the ROMEO AND JULIET WINDMILL, constructed in 1897.

It was a fifty-six-foot tall tower with a fourteen-foot wheel at the top. The structure's shape made it an especially memorable example of both Wright's design and his eccentricity (the latter was demonstrated as well by his installation in the 1930s of a loudspeaker at the top of the tower to broadcast Bach and Beethoven to the cows and the farm workers).

In plan the structure is an octagon from which a slightly taller "storm prow" (Wright's name) protrudes at the top and on one side. This diamond shape faces into the prevailing southwest winds, slicing through them to diminish their force on the tall building. Consisting of four-inch-square vertical posts covered with sheathing

The structures at the Midway Farm were utilitarian buildings but Wright could never pass up an opportunity to leave his personal imprint. The spire on the milk tower is the keynote here, a geometric abstraction topped by a working weathervane.

and board-and-batten siding, the wooden superstructure was secured to its base of stone and stiffened with iron rods.

Wright took to calling the structure the Romeo and Juliet Windmill, a recognition of the symbolism implied by its design. It is easy enough to imagine Wright smiling at the moniker, given the manner in which the octagon embraces (or is penetrated by?) the diamond.

The aunts saw the added investment in the tower—a commonplace steel windmill performing the same function would have cost less than a third as much—as "becoming to the dignity of the beloved school." The freedom the aunts gave their nephew subjected them to some derision. Their brothers, Wright's formidable and practical uncles Enos, Jenkin, James, John, and Thomas, said it "looked expensive and foolish." They predicted it would blow down, but one could hardly blame any hard-working farmer who happened by for mocking so strange a design when a utilitarian windmill was all that had been asked for.

Looking backward in time, we can recognize easily today that the Romeo and Juliet Windmill is Wright at his iconic and iconoclastic best. The current tower is a reconstruction; several restoration attempts, including one by Wright, failed to stabilize it, so in 1990 the structure was dismantled and rebuilt. The stone base is original, and much of the roof was also salvaged.

The simplest building on the Taliesin property, TAN-Y-DERI, is recognizable as an American foursquare. Wright designed it in 1907 for his sister and brother-in-law, Jane and Andrew T. Porter, when they returned to the valley for Porter to manage the Hillside Home School. Tan-Y-Deri is in the shadow of the Romeo and Juliet Windmill.

Tan-Y-Deri grew from the same inspiration as a design Wright had done on commission for the April 1907 issue of *Ladies' Home Journal*: "A Fireproof House for $5000." It is a simple house, yet deceptively rich in Wright touches, among them the siting, the massive limestone chimney mass, the horizontal siding (the

result of a 1930s rethinking by Wright, replacing the original shingles), and the low pyramidal hip roof (an echo of his favored hip roofs which, in larger prairie style houses, were elaborated into multiple hips of various sizes and heights).

The foursquare, as embodied in Tan-Y-Deri, is by far the most copied of Wright's designs. Its stolid, practical configuration suited many and varied sites, rural and urban, and required little design or construction skill to adapt. This is a building that Wright might well have let drop from his sleeve (as he liked to say), one that lacks fussy details but embodies a number of his essential tenets. Today it is a residence for Taliesin fellows and apprentices.

THE MIDWAY FARM, located about halfway between the house and Hillside School, was a remodeling of a farm complex. In 1938, Wright linked several older buildings together, integrating dormitory space with silos, a milk room, and machine sheds, mingling the life of the farm with that of the Fellowship.

The complex sits in the lap of Midway Hill behind it. In designing the long, horizontal structure, Wright managed to retain the austere beauty of plain farm buildings while adding decorative ornamentation. The broad, low planes of the barns have the dignity of functional buildings; the varied, overlapping roof planes, like those at the house, match the surrounding ridges.

The state of the Midway Farm today reflects the changes at Taliesin in the last half-century. The life of the farm was long inseparable from life at Taliesin, especially during the Depression when vegetables, milk, cheese, eggs, chicken, beef, and animal fodder were essential to survival. Later, in the 1950s when Wright's practice flourished, the energies of the apprentices shifted to architecture and they no longer worked the farm. The tumbledown appearance of the buildings reflects that change, with roofless silos, missing siding, and the empty feeling of a farm after the cows have been auctioned.

"A farmstead here is somehow warmed and given life by the red of the barns," Wright wrote in 1930. "Wisconsin, fond of passing laws, should pass another law compelling every farmer to paint his barn red." Wright loved and understood barns and it shows at the Midway Farm.

Today, Taliesin is a place undergoing restoration. In 1988, the Governor's Commission on Taliesin was established by Governor Tommy Thompson. The following year a report was issued that led to the creation of the nonprofit Taliesin Preservation Commission, which has recently been renamed Taliesin Preservation, Inc. Independent of the Frank Lloyd Wright Foundation (though a number of the Foundation's trustees double as Commission board members), Taliesin Preservation, Inc., raises funds, operates the public tours, and conducts the preservation efforts in alliance with the Frank Lloyd Wright Foundation.

Wright had little interest in western oil painting, but this portrait of his mother came with him from the Home and Studio and today hangs over the massive fireplace in the Taliesin studio. Wright himself commissioned the painting and insisted that the subject wear period dress—not the clothing she wore daily at the turn-of-the-century when the work was executed, but frontier garb (of Wright's design) that resembled clothing her immigrant parents had worn when they arrived from Wales. In a sense, Wright stage managed his own version of "Whistler's mother"—except that, unlike Charles McNeil Whistler's, it wasn't an aesthetic arrangement in black and gray but a rare moment of nostalgia.

The work done to date has included the conversion of the Spring Green Restaurant (a work completed after Wright's death) into a visitor's center and book shop for Taliesin; the reconstruction of the Romeo and Juliet Windmill; and the preparation of basic studies of each of the buildings, historic structure reports (or HSRs as they are informally known). These documents include precise recording of the fabric of each structure *in situ* as well as historical analysis of what was done and when in building and remodeling. Drawing upon documentary as well as physical evidence, the studies aim to establish a building chronology. Fund raising is another challenge: the estimated cost for the restoration efforts is in the tens of millions of dollars.

Yet in preserving Taliesin there lies an unavoidable trap. The main goal of the effort has been to preserve the site for future generations: To visit Taliesin is to better understand Wright and his work. But preservation involves change, ranging from simple maintenance of materials to significant reconstruction to correct not only what time has eroded but also shoddy construction due to too little money, inexperienced workmanship, or simple human error.

In place more than a century, the Romeo and Juliet windmill has become very much a part—an *organic* part—of its landscape.

Wright always had an angle, his thinking always had an edge. Consider the waterfall at Taliesin. He dammed a stream, thereby creating a pond that was both pleasing to the eye and useful for controlling the flow of water to nearby fields. Yet he located the dam so the rumble of the falling water could be heard from the house but was just out of sight (though the visitor approaching the house got a memorable drive-by view). In that way, the inhabitants never got so accustomed to seeing the dam that they took it for granted. The rumble of the waterfall is thus part of the audible experience at Taliesin, a tease and a surprise. Wright was in control, managing his natural and built environment.

Wright's shadow looms over these efforts. His presence is palpable at Taliesin and changing anything is to risk reducing that presence. This is true philosophically as well. After all, his notion of organic architecture implied change and nowhere was that truer than at Taliesin, which by accident and intention was forever evolving. Wright frequently changed walls and rearranged terraces, furniture, and art; one of the last drawings off his board before his death was for another remodeling scheme.

As far as Wright was concerned, Taliesin was never finished. Unlike the Home and Studio, where Wright himself froze the calendar with his departure in 1909, there is no one obvious date to assign to Taliesin as the target for a restoration. Wright's death in 1959 might seem the logical moment, but more than a few historians believe Taliesin's heyday was twenty years before that, in the mid-1930s. Such lines drawn in the sands of history are ever-so-temporary thanks to the tides of time. At Taliesin, there is nothing more intriguing than the omnipresent evidence of the designer's brain at work. This is a house that has seen more remodeling than a decade of shelter magazines. About Taliesin there is a sense of improvisation, of wit, of problem solving, of experiment. Preserving it thus presents an unprecedented array of questions.

As Wright explained, Taliesin's program was to be "an abstract combination of stone and wood, as they naturally met in the aspect of the hills around about." When we visited Taliesin in November of 1997 to shoot the first of the photographs shown in these pages, the living quarters of the house were empty. The members of the Taliesin Fellowship had already relocated to Phoenix for the winter (the utopian experiment that Wright established still divides its time between Wisconsin and Arizona).

Despite its emptiness, Taliesin that day was a place in which Wright was eerily present. At the center of the inner courtyard was the tea circle where he held court; Wright liked nothing better than an audience willing to hang on his every word. It is easy to imagine him surrounded by apprentices, the center of a perpetual charrette. As the sun rose, it illuminated the façade of the house looking outward into the biting wind. Hours later, clouds would roll in and bring a blanket of early snow, but in the sidelong morning light we admired the extraordinary bird walk.

If it were necessary to single out one element of Taliesin as its most dramatic, it would have to be the bird walk. The defiance of gravity was a key attribute of Wright's work. He was always testing the limits of the building practices of his time (the debate at Fallingwater about the cantilevers is well into its seventh decade and shows no sign of resolution). The bird walk is not a place for acrophobes: the sensation of being suspended in space is borne of knowledge (you saw it on approach, of course; Wright planned that) and of distance (it is a full forty feet long, extended by Wright at Olgivanna's request).

In the way that early American construction was characterized by the post and beam, Wright's was characterized by the cantilever. Examples abound beyond the Fallingwater porches and the bird walk. Early in his career he began designing broad overhangs into his Oak Park buildings. There is also a tenon-like protuberance from the master bedroom at Wingspread in Wisconsin, the residence built for Herbert ("Hib") Johnson. Numerous other examples can be found in just a cursory look at his work.

At Taliesin, the bird walk is a terrace disguised. It resembles nothing more than a great diving board despite the short walls around the perimeter. Symbolically, to use a cliché of our day, it's very much "out there," a cantilevered walkway built amid the limbs of ancient oaks. Wright himself took pride in being "out there," taking chances, challenging the standards of his profession and the expectations of his clients. The greatest challenge facing Taliesin's caretakers is to preserve the spirit of that restless empiricism.

Wright periodically left Taliesin to supervise construction of his projects. When returning from Tokyo and his Imperial Hotel, he brought back Japanese prints, sculptures, and other artifacts, many of which still decorate the house. During the slow days of the 1920s when his career seemed in eclipse and during the heady days after his face looked out from the cover of *Time*, he always came back. He proudly proclaimed that it was "Wisconsin [that] put sap into my veins." That was the romanticized view he adopted as an adult but, in a more candid moment with Taliesin fellow Edgar Tafel, he remembered childhood chores on the farm as "all pulling tits and shoveling shit."

Taliesin came to represent for Wright and, later, the Fellowship, an idealized pastoral existence. In Wright's life and writings, little is as it seems, however. Wright gradually acquired what had been a handful of separate farms owned by members of the Lloyd Jones clan, thanks to his mother, his aunts, and, in later years, his own growing affluence. Taliesin was run as a dairy farm with a herd of Guernseys that the apprentices helped care for and that, along with the vegetable garden and the chickens, provided essential foodstuffs during the Depression. Yet, even the cows, whether Guernseys or Holsteins, were a component in his larger vision of the Taliesin property, design elements that complemented the agricultural character of the site. Wright himself was known to work the fields well into his sixties and took pleasure in occasionally operating tractors and other farm machinery. He also relished living the good life with minions to prepare and serve his meals. Elaborate entertainments were regular events, with dramatic and musical performances and formal meals. This was true in lean times as well as prosperous ones. The famous came to visit–Carl Sandburg, Charles Lindbergh, Claire Booth Luce, Ludwig Mies van der Rohe, Charles Laughton, and countless others–and surely many commissions came to him thanks to the impression left by the noble house that was Taliesin when the lord was alive and in residence. Then he would be off, touring the immediate countryside or driving across the country, always in the prestige car of the day: at different times, he owned a Knox roadster, a Cadillac phaeton, a Cord, a Lincoln zephyr, a Packard straight-eight, a Mercedes sedan, and a Jaguar coupe, as well as a range of lesser cars such as Crosleys, Dodges, and a Hillman. Many of these vehicles were painted Cherokee red, although Wright's son John remembered Wright's first car, one of the first to arrive in Oak Park, as a distinct yellow. It was a 1910 Stoddard-Dayton sports roadster, its body modified at the factory to a Wright design. "The good citizens of Oak Park called it the Yellow Devil," remembered John Wright, "and not many days passed before the Oak Park police threatened to confiscate it. The speed law was 25 miles an hour. The Yellow Devil could go 60." Wright took matters of style very seriously, and making an entrance and exit was part of the drama, as was the mode of transport. Traveling well was part of living well.

Wright liked having it both ways: He was a man of the earth and lord of the big house. Yet he was no autocrat; most apprentices recall their time at the Fellowship with warmth and remember Wright as an extraordinarily alive, creative, and available presence. Perhaps it is symbolic (or even "organic") that he liked nothing better than an impromptu picnic.

If the Home and Studio was Wright's laboratory during the years of the prairie style, Taliesin was the fulcrum of his mature career. After being banished from Oak Park and returning to Spring Green, he created a home that, rather than closing off the suburban streetscapes outside, began welcoming the open vistas of the terrain around him. Like the Home and Studio, Taliesin can be "read," detail by detail, for Wright's history: the changes he made over time, the stonework, the cantilever. Taliesin is truly his "natural house" and, together with the way he used (and modified) the natural attributes of the land, it is the embodiment of his philosophy of organic architecture.

Taliesin West, observed across the oasis of water and vegetation that defines its principal façade.

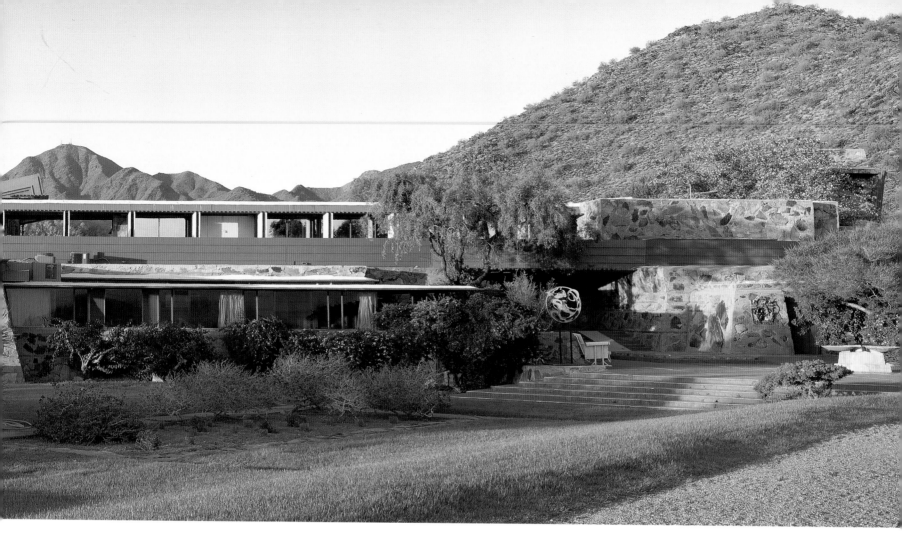

III TALIE/IN WE/T
/cottsdale, Arizona

In 1954, Philip Johnson said of Wright that he was "the greatest architect of the nineteenth century." Much later, Johnson felt compelled to justify his dismissive description, explaining that it had been coined decades earlier when he and Wright had been involved in an imbroglio over Wright's inclusion in a museum show, the landmark 1932 *Modern Architecture: International Exhibition* at the Museum of Modern Art in New York.

A fit of pique may well explain how the savvy Johnson could be so wrong-headed as to dismiss Wright's later work, yet his flippant remark does contain a useful half-truth. Not only did Wright's career begin *in* but his early work was very much *of* the nineteenth century. The shingle style residence in Oak Park demolished no

Though the access road is roughly a mile long, the Eagle Stone marks the spot at which the buildings come into view. This standing stone on its conglomerate plinth is both a portent of the buildings ahead and a respectful reference to the ancient peoples who came before.

A visitor approaching by foot rather than by car follows a circuitous path that wends through dense desert vegetation.

precedents and, by the 1930s, even the prairie style might have seemed to Johnson mannered or old-fashioned. Wright was certainly seen by many observers as over the hill.

Wright was written off more than once in his long career (even by himself, as his personal historiography involved rewriting the facts of his life, with himself often cast as someone who constantly had to overcome adversity and philistinism). In truth, the ever-resourceful Wright did manage to reinvent himself and his work repeatedly. The prairie house, the textile-block house, the Usonian house, as well as such unique buildings as the Johnson Wax Administration Building, Fallingwater, and the Guggenheim Museum, all offer ample evidence of his ability to recast his architectural approach. He was able, again and again, to suit the zeitgeist of new eras, all the while assembling the extraordinarily varied oeuvre that today seems to have survived as some sort of personal ziggurat awing visitors and winning new and often youthful converts–among them Philip Johnson, whose more recent pronouncements put him clearly in the camp of Wright's advocates. All of that said, no reinvention was more dramatic than that of Taliesin West.

The uncluttered pale blue sky of the desert displays the rusty reds and browns and gray-greens of the desert.

The Frank Lloyd Wright Foundation today retains some 600 acres, allowing a generous margin of desert to surround the compound. Wildlife remains plentiful: not only rabbits and birds but, as visitors are warned, rattle snakes and scorpions.

From the south-
east, Taliesin West
appears to be a
fortress emerging
from the desert.

The simplicity of the construction, exemplified here
by the viga-like tails of the
beams, blends with the antediluvian feel of the desert
vegetation.

Immediately behind Taliesin West is Maricopa Hill, elevation 1900 feet.

The central walk is the main artery at Taliesin, shown here from the dining room (the glass enclosed room on the left), past the bell tower, and on to the drafting room (middle distance, to the left of the pergola).

The view north from the Sunset Terrace, through the loggia, along the slightly canted north-south axis of the complex. The McDowell Mountains are at the rear of Taliesin West, Wright's private quarters on the right on this image.

A never-to-be-built resort hotel was its harbinger. In 1927, Dr. Alexander Chandler, a veterinarian-turned-hotelier, had a strange idea for a Venetian-inspired hotel. Although Venice without water would seem to be a contradiction in terms, the hard-driving Chandler nevertheless commissioned Wright to design his San Marcos in the Desert. In January of 1928, Chandler wired Wright, inviting him to come to Arizona to execute the extravagant hotel design on site. No further inducement was required to convince Wright to abandon snowbound Taliesin and its sub-zero temperatures, so he loaded up his Packard touring car and headed south, together with his "family," which then consisted of Olgivanna, Iovanna, Svetlana, and the "boys," the apprentices of the nascent Fellowship.

    Wright could ill afford to pay for accommodations for his entourage, so he prevailed upon Chandler to allow him to construct what he termed an "ephemerid," a temporary camp on a rocky plateau overlooking the site of the proposed hotel. The compound became more formally known as Ocatillo (the name was also spelled Ocatilla). It was a very casual place, consisting of a dozen-odd cabins built of wood-

Wright added imaginative touches to his "desert masonry." Here he improvised string courses, though with a typical Wrightian inversion. What seem at first like string courses are really voids, long horizontal depressions in the masonry. Note, too, the geometric rail above.

The previous inhabitants of Maricopa Mesa left Wright a virtual signpost which he happily incorporated into his landscape. The incised stones on the left (note there are two, cemented together) are petroglyphs made by the Hohokum Indians.

en platforms with partial walls and canvas roofs. The wood was painted a dull red, said to have been inspired by the rosy hue of the desert.

The little community proved even more temporary than expected. An anticipated return for the winter of 1929-1930 never happened, as the stock market crash of 1929 stalled all progress on the hotel. Dr. Chandler never fully recovered from the financial setbacks sustained in the 1929 crash, and the hotel became nothing more than an unfulfilled dream. Yet the lessons of the camp that was Ocatillo later proved valuable. Just as the first Taliesin in Spring Green had more than one incarnation, Ocatillo was the preliminary template upon which Wright would later elaborate Taliesin West.

Although the Taliesin Fellowship was established in 1932, well before Taliesin West was begun, the Arizona complex is the truest architectural expression of the Fellowship. Yet what triggered its establishment was actually a case of pneumonia.

The notion of permanent winter quarters for the Fellowship in Arizona had been pursued for some years, but the right property at the right price had not been found. Wright's reinvigorated career had also kept him

From a vantage at the western end of the drafting room looking south over the prow terrace, the viewer can sense something of the unique angularity of Taliesin West.

Today's visitor to Taliesin West first encounters a monolith of desert masonry, the "Light Tower" that Wright designed in 1947. It pitches at a fifteen-degree angle from the vertical (the roof trusses are fifteen degrees, horizontal), and features the Wrightian symbol for the Fellowship, a double-square spiral. Along with the bubbling fountain, each of these elements symbolizes Wright conquering the desert.

busier than ever and he gloried in his new successes. Then, in December of 1936, as he approached his seventieth birthday, he was suddenly reminded that he wasn't as ageless as he sometimes seemed. A prolonged bout with pneumonia led his doctors to advise him to find a more clement climate in which to spend the winter months. Within a year, Wright took the title to eight hundred acres in the Paradise Valley in Scottsdale, Arizona, in the shadow of the McDowell Mountains. In January of 1938, he and a band of Taliesin fellows established a temporary encampment there in the Sonoran Desert for the winter months. Thereafter, Wright led an annual migration to Taliesin West, and from roughly November to April the desert camp in Scottsdale would become home.

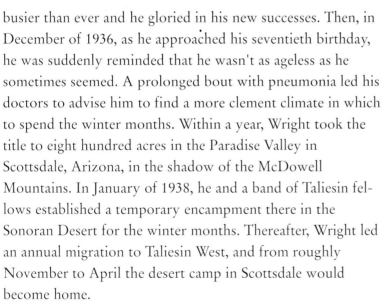

To understand Taliesin West one must understand the Fellowship. Wright's goal wasn't to open an architecture school. The Fellowship's purpose was larger. Sculptors, painters, and musicians were to be a part of the Fellowship. Everyone participated in theater, music, and dance, regularly producing elaborate spectacles with colorful costumes and sets. Wright was always the gray eminence, Olgivanna at his side, dispensing approval and his philosophy of architecture and life to the community of admirers around him.

One ritual in particular, "The Box," is symbolic of the admixture of creativity and personality cult that was the Fellowship. In preparing for it, each apprentice would execute drawings for a pet project. The drawings were then presented to Wright in a special box made for the occasion by one of the apprentices. These ceremonial events were usually held at Christmas and at Wright's birthday. He would then open the box to examine the drawings within, and critique the apprentices' work *en masse*.

Olgivanna's earlier years at Gurdjieff's Institute for the Harmonious Development of Man was also an important influence. The highly structured and multidisciplined existence at the Fellowship resembled the communal life at the Institute. Gurdjieff's spiritual component became, in the world according to Wright, a logical

In the foreground is the "prow," as Wright named the protruding triangular terrace that points south toward Scottsdale and Phoenix. The nautical choice of words, together with the use of sail-cloth for the original roofing material, brings to mind a sense of the building as a paradoxical ship on the desert.

Looking northwest along the main axis of the shaded exterior walkway, the view is defined by the bold trusswork of a pergola with the main entrance at its vanishing point. Like traditional Spanish Colonial architecture, interior spaces at Taliesin West tend to open to the exterior rather than to hallways; in the same way, the buildings are for the most part only one room deep.

Viewed from the rear garden, the spine of the 1956 Music Pavilion defines the rear boundary of the built complex at Taliesin.

extension of Wright's organic architecture, in which buildings were to be in unity and harmony with nature. Gurdjieff himself, a charismatic, Buddha-like figure with a large, shaven head, visited Taliesin on several occasions and Wright once compared him to Gandhi. Both the Fellowship and the Institute relied on physical disciplines to enhance perception; yet the parallels only go so far. The Institute's focus was on "The Work", the seeking of individual spiritual harmony. At the Taliesins, the goal was also the work—the work of the Master, Frank Lloyd Wright.

Taliesin West is a campsite made permanent. The working drawings done for its construction were surprisingly haphazard; to this day, full plans do not exist. Wright improvised his drawings on butcher paper as the stone and sand that would be used to fabricate the walls were being collected by apprentices. (The brown paper was less reflective of the sun's glare, a practical attribute for drafting done in direct sunlight.) Quarters for Mr. and Mrs. Wright were built first. Called the Sun Trap, it was little more than a wood-and-canvas cubicle atop a concrete slab.

The complex as outlined in 1938 is recognizable in the buildings that survive to this day, save for various peripheral structures, some of which postdate Wright's death. Whatever its impromptu quality, however, Taliesin West was not built in a single season. No doubt ideas for the place had been percolating through Wright's brain for a decade and, like Taliesin and the Home and Studio, the complex at Scottsdale continued to be a place for

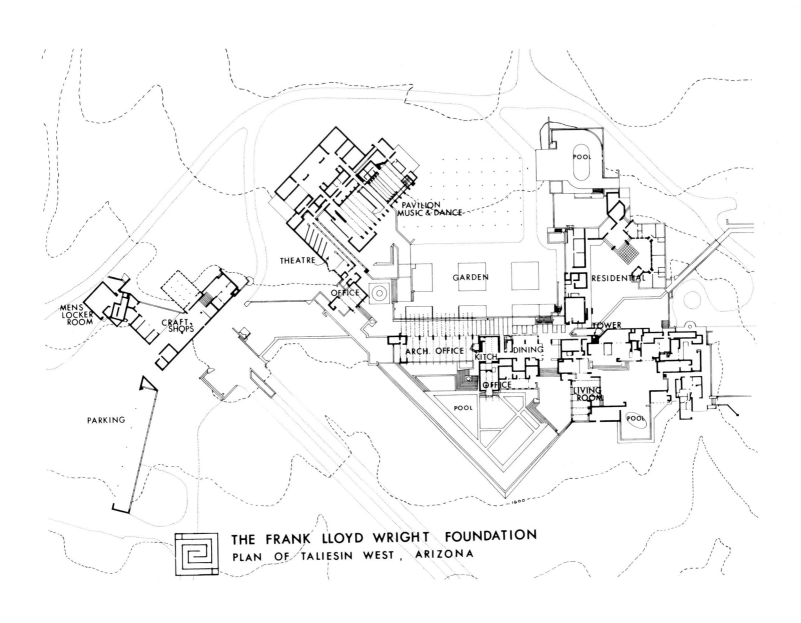

THE FRANK LLOYD WRIGHT FOUNDATION
PLAN OF TALIESIN WEST, ARIZONA

Art Center College of Design
Library
1700 Lida Street
Pasadena, Calif. 91103

experimentation as long as Wright was in residence. The first phase of construction required roughly four years to complete, from the winter of 1938 through the spring of 1941. Each year thereafter when the caravan of cars and vans would arrive from Spring Green for the winter months, Wright would soon devise marching orders for his merry band. To this day, members of the Fellowship who survive from Wright's time talk of his bursts of creativity, of the renovations he devised on arrival. After months away from the place, he brought to his return what he liked to call "the fresh eye." As Tom Casey, a longtime Taliesin fellow remarked in a recent interview, "He was never content to stop fussing, to stop changing."

From the start, the Arizona setting made new demands on Wright, but he demonstrated that the basic tenets of his philosophy of architecture could be universally applied; Taliesin West may actually be his best exemplar. The enclosures he required were varied. One would house him and his immediate family; another would be a workroom for drafting and teaching. There was a detached office/study for Wright, communal areas for the kitchen and dining room, and spaces for musical and film entertainments. All were to be integrated into the natural features of the arid mesa.

Wright always rose to the challenge of designing a theater. In his inimical way, Wright reversed the emphasis by making the audience space in the Music Pavilion as theatrical as the stage itself.

Once a part of the loggia or breezeway that separated Wright's private quarters from community spaces, the dining room was later enclosed with glass. Note the chairs: they are based on a design Wright made for the Midway Gardens in Chicago before World War I, adopted for Taliesin West in the 1960s after Wright's death.

In broad strokes, he created an T-shaped exterior "hallway." The leg of the T ran more or less east-west, extending from Wright's office at the northwest end to his private quarters at the opposite end, running alongside the largest space in the complex, the drafting room, and common spaces for kitchen and dining. The top of the T was another open artery that ran from the front to the rear of the complex, passing through a breezeway or loggia that separated the Wright family living quarters from the central core of the community. To the rear of the main structure was a movie theater and gallery and quarters for apprentices with their own enclosed courtyard. The structures were set upon an angular footprint of concrete pads that defined terraces and gardens as well as foundations for the low masonry walls.

When Taliesin West was completed, Wright as usual wasn't bashful about describing his accomplishment. "Our new desert camp belong[s] to the Arizona desert as though it had stood there during creation." His words weren't mere braggadocio.

In period photographs of the place rising from the desert floor during construction, the stone plinths emerging from their wooden forms look like some strange composite of neolithic standing stones and ancient

In Mr. Wright's office the rough stone walls define the space, grooved to soften their mass, while the translucent ceilings welcome the light from above.

The garden room has evolved into an event space for the Fellowship, accommodating parties small and large. Since the room's construction in 1940, fixed windows have been added, allowing for air conditioning, as well as views of the mountains to the north.

The largest space in the complex, the drafting room is more than one hundred feet long. As at any other up-to-date firm or architectural school, the drafting tables have, for the most part, been superceded by computer screens.

In a casual way, this image contains many of the elements that characterize Taliesin West. Most important is the way in which the interior space cannot be separated from the outdoors, but in addition there's a small sampling of artifacts, a piano, and the rubble wall that, again, emphasizes the essential connection between the inside and outside.

ruins. Atop the great canted buttresses were mounted the roof trusses, with canvas stretched between them, lapping and slapping in the breezes. The effect was to be light, airy, and translucent, conveying the same sense of openness that the canvas tents at Ocatillo had done. Each of the elements was rudimentary in the extreme: rubble stone, poured concrete, rough-sawn redwood, and coarse fabric. Taken together, they were elemental, the embodiment of the building act, a solid foundation and stiff frame below offering safety and security, with ample light and ventilation from above.

Taliesin West was quite unlike Taliesin–how could it not be, given the difference in climate? There were no gables or hips, the roofs were just sloping shed roofs, typically at a flattened fifteen degrees. At both Taliesins, the pitch of the roofs mimed the surrounding landscape; at Scottsdale, the visual echo was of the slopes of the nearby McDowell Mountains. From a distance, Taliesin West gave the observer a sense of belonging to the landscape.

One construction decision crucial to the site-specific character of the place concerned the walls. To a contemporary builder, the method Wright devised for building the stone walls seemed outlandish. The raw material was on site: on arriving there, the Fellowship found quantities of volcanic rock, a colorful rubble with tones of

umber, blue, and purple. Wright instructed that wooden forms be built, most of them trapezoidal in section, wider at the bottom than at the top (though some cant out above a waistline, while others are strictly vertical). Within the forms, the larger stones would be set flat side out, with large boulders used as fill in the center. Smaller stones and a thin mix of concrete were then poured into the forms to cement the stones together, producing an aggregate. When the forms were removed, cement obscuring the faces of the large stones was chipped away by hand and the stone acid-washed, producing what Wright termed "desert masonry rubble walls."

To the well-trained mason, the haphazard quality is an affront to craftsmanship; yet these walls were not built by craftsmen but by novice apprentices. The end result also bears an indisputable resemblance to the texture and colors of the surrounding mountains and canyons. The effect is enhanced by the framework above, consisting of trusses of rough-sawn wood, with knots visible. With this exposed skeleton, the roof structures seem to assume prehistoric shapes–Wright called them "strange firm forms"–as the jags of the trusses, their odd angles aligning and casting peculiar shadows, stand forth like the standing ribs of an ancient, sun-dried beast.

The final touch was the expanse of canvas between the brown-stained redwood beams. Individual sheets of canvas were stretched over wooden frames and then mounted as panels, some of them slidable. Just as sections of

Viewed from the gardens, the horizontal line of Taliesin West's rear elevation is broken by its water tower. Reminiscent of bell towers on early Spanish missions, it encloses a bell whose tolling still defines the day's schedule at Taliesin West, ringing for meal times and scheduled events.

Another of the standing stones, this one defining a garden corner.

the roofs were movable, walls flaps functioned as doors and windows, opening and closing to encourage air flow during the heat of the day and to retain warmth during the cold desert nights.

In the early days, the place had the look of a camp: a temporary settlement but one in which an ingenious pioneer spirit was in charge. In photographs from the 1930s, apprentices always seem to be wearing tool belts, wielding pickaxes, or carrying shovels. The rubble stone walls anchored the roof trusses which, in turn, framed the great horizontal sails. Taken together, the elements had an antediluvian feel: it was a mad, hunkered-down response to the rays of the sun that beat down mercilessly.

The buildings at Taliesin West are set low to the ground like so many of Wright's design. There are deep over-hangs and bands of horizontal openings. There are a number of his one-legged fireplaces, stone hearths that look old enough to have warmed a caveman. The temptation is to draw parallels to other works, but that would be to risk missing the specialness of the place. It is unique in the oeuvre of a man whose works frequently stood out for their originality.

Looking north, the view is of the rear court and garden, through which the apprentice quarters are reached. Yet these grand stairs also suggest access not so much to buildings but to the desert and mountains of which Taliesin West is a outgrowth.

The palette is fixed: the red painted surfaces, the ferrous reds of the rocks in the wall, the fading greys and greens of the concrete and desert plants.

Hummingbirds make a sort of purring sound while they hover, visiting the tall desert flowers in the court yard garden behind the main building.

If any of Wright's buildings can be said to be even remotely Gothic, Taliesin West is the best candidate given its asymmetrical, fortress-like quality.

Perhaps the biggest surprise of all about Taliesin West is that the buildings, at least as originally conceived, had essentially no traditional windows. Natural light poured in through the canvas roofs; side flaps allowed free access for breezes. Over time, clerestory windows were incorporated into private quarters, and walls were glazed in order to accommodate air conditioning, a compromise made necessary when Taliesin West ceased to be solely a winter encampment and became a year-round home for some members of the Wright organization. But in its first incarnation Taliesin West was a windowless place.

Another attribute that adds to its specialness is what might be called its archaeology. It isn't truly an exercise in archaeology, yet the shards of pots, grinding stones, and even petroglyphs (inscribed rocks) that Wright and company found on the site indicated that the Maricopa Mesa had been used much earlier by the native Hohokum Indians. For Wright, these added a mystical quality to the landscape and, always economical in building his own structures, he happily incorporated the decorative and incantatory prehistoric finds into his work. One is at the prow, another at the beginning of the pergola. Today ethnologists would frown upon such out-of-context recycling of pre-Columbian artifacts, but Wright's intention certainly was to honor and respect the holiness of the objects.

It's fashionable to talk of architecture in terms of negative space, of voids rather than volumes. In the same way, then, Taliesin West cannot be appreciated without a sensitivity to the shadows it casts as the blazing sun makes its circuit.

Another peculiarity of Taliesin West is that it was built by unskilled labor. While it is an acknowledged landmark in twentieth-century architecture, for much of its existence it was built and maintained by a series of young men and women with little or no training in the building trades. That certainly contributed to its handmade character, as did Wright's tight budget in the early days in Arizona. If Taliesin was a stage set, as Wright remarked, where he might perform for his potential clients, then Taliesin West was more like a bivouac, a seasonal escape from the life of a performer.

The key characteristic that distinguishes Taliesin West is its geometry. The shapes are quite different from those at Taliesin or the Home and Studio or, for that matter, those of traditional architecture. Wright resisted the pull of the rectilinear in Scottsdale, electing instead to rely upon the angles of triangles and trapezoids. In some measure, this is a reflection once again of his drafting tools, which included the standard right isosceles triangle, with its pair of forty-five degree angles, and the elongated right triangle with thirty- and sixty-degree angles. The acute angles and obliquities of Taliesin West help give the place a new degree of indirectness, a characteristic Wright sought increasingly to give his buildings. (It should be noted that the earliest known plan for Taliesin West is thick with right angles; only as Wright experienced the site did he shift the emphasis to the openness of oblique

angles.) The result is the incorporation of the extraordinary vistas around Taliesin West into the structures as no set of blocky boxes could have done.

Accepting its uniqueness, comparisons become inevitable, and the contrast between the Taliesins is telling. The rubble-wall desert masonry wouldn't have worked in Wisconsin. The stone was different, as were the color and texture of the landscape. More to the point, the freeze-and-thaw cycle in the north would have destroyed such walls in a few winters. The roofing system also would have been absurd there. But in Arizona it all works.

If Taliesin is a winter coat–stylish, imaginatively cut and tailored, but with its collar up to seal out cold breezes and ensure privacy, then, in comparison, Taliesin West is more like a beach ensemble, a bathing suit, beach towel, and umbrella, with stones at hand for a bonfire at sunset. This was not merely a matter of adapting to a different climate: Taliesin encircles itself, while Taliesin West is open to the expanse of the overheated desert that surrounds it.

The buildings seem to crouch as if trying to get out of the sun.

Wright's haven in Scottsdale cannot be taken in at a glance. Or even on one visit.

Taliesin West today is headquarters for the Frank Lloyd Wright Foundation, which consists of the Frank Lloyd Wright Archives, the Frank Lloyd Wright School of Architecture, and Taliesin Architects. The Foundation owns the buildings; the Archives houses a research facility for scholars; and Taliesin Architects functions as a for-profit subsidiary that is heir to Wright's architectural firm and offers a range of design services, including the controversial "Unbuilt Program," which markets modified versions of Wright's unexecuted designs.

The buildings themselves have changed since Wright's death in 1959, just as they changed in the twenty-plus years of his occupancy. The principal caretaker, Olgivanna, and the Foundation have allowed the place to evolve. She enlarged her quarters; a building was built for the archives. That evolution continues, as a new visitor's center is planned for a designated site using a design devised by Taliesin Architects. Not surprisingly, it will resemble the other buildings. One might characterize it as in the vernacular, the Wrightian architectural language he evolved specifically for Taliesin West, using the trapezoidal walls of stone immersed in concrete and the angled roof trusses.

Work is being done daily at Taliesin West by architects, instructors, students, administrators, and tour guides. That is as it should be: Wright would hardly have wanted the place to be enshrined as if in a bell jar. The canvas roofs and side flaps from Wright's day are gone, a change that has radically altered the experience of the

place. The temporary nature of the original structures has given way to a greater sense of permanence. Many of the trusses are steel. The canvas has been replaced by succeeding generations of other materials, most recently by an acrylic and fiberglass product that contains an air space. These more permanent panels have made the installation of air-conditioning systems possible but have also changed the nature of the buildings as the panels, though translucent, lack the flex of the diaphanous canvas. In its original incarnation, the roofs must have seemed almost alive, while today the rigid plastic seems fossilized.

A more dramatic change has occurred to the environs of Taliesin West. The prow was an oasis and it remains much as it was in Wright's day, a tiny lawn and small pool in the foreground backed by cacti sticking up like fingers here and there, amid the fragile vegetation of the desert floor. But as the eye moves deeper into the middle distance, the high-tension power lines appear, with towers linked by a skein of wires. In 1951, Wright threatened to sell out and move because the great ugly swags of power lines had been strung across his desert vista. Little could he have known how they would power development in Phoenix, bringing electricity from Roosevelt Dam.

On the left, the overhanging trusses protect the cave-like portal of the original dining room while, at center, the upper level is an open porch called the "guest deck," which welcomes breezes and offers a panoramic view of the Paradise Valley.

When Wright arrived his little community was isolated, an outpost about a dozen miles from what is now Scottsdale, on unincorporated land. Scottsdale itself was a small town, with a population of about one thousand; it is more than a hundred times larger today. In the more immediate vicinity of Taliesin West there was little except a couple of minor horse and sheep ranches. In those days, Taliesin West was an oasis in the traditional sense, a patch of fertile green amid an expanse of arid desert. That has changed.

Today little desert survives between Taliesin West and Scottsdale, and what does is largely within the boundaries of Taliesin West itself. The acreage that surrounds the core complex is a desert buffer of cactus and sand that not only Wright but a hundred generations of Native Americans would recognize as natural. Beyond the bounds of Taliesin West's preserve, however, the Sonoran Desert has been consumed by the tapestry of suburban civilization, a reminder that Taliesin West's front yard has become a metropolitan area populated by millions. The shifting sands are unrecognizable beneath the imposed grid of streets, structures, and California gardens made possible by the network of irrigation canals. The delicate ecological balance has been lost: irrigation has made everything more lush and people who once went there to escape allergens now find its air dense with pollens.

In a paradoxical reversal Wright would have decried, the unspoiled desert environs that buffer Taliesin West have become the oasis, a small reminder of what has been lost. Wright once remarked of his acres in Scottsdale that they offered him "a look over the rim of the world." Were he alive to gaze out upon that view today, he would not recognize the vista, as it has become the explosion of growth that is greater Phoenix, where

the population has more than doubled since his death. As Wright scholar Neil Levine wisely wrote, "The closer civilization comes—and it is extremely close by now—the more Taliesin West seems to have to say."

Today's out-of-state visitors arrive, for the most part, by air, looking down from their little airborne portholes. Air travel allows visitors a sense of domination as they descend over the Rockies. In contrast, Wright arrived more humbly (not that he was ever particularly humble). His approach was by land, in a car that was part of a convoy traveling from Wisconsin. In the 1930s when the annual treks began, much of Route 66 wasn't even paved. He had to make his way through the mountains, driving over the rugged ridges that, from the air, pose no obstacle. Wright's response to the challenge of the environment was to create one of his most enduring and admired monuments.

Taliesin West is one of his least accessible buildings, however, one that critics and historians have tended to neglect, an inconvenient deviation from the main stream of his work. Yet for those who experience it, Taliesin

Taliesin West as the sun sets.

West is certainly among his most satisfying.

Taliesin West should not be understood as a dwelling. It is a campus, a seasonal escape constructed for Wright, his family, and the Fellowship. Unlike the original Taliesin in Wisconsin, which was conceived as a home for Wright and his lover, Mamah Borthwick, and only later evolved into the headquarters for Wright's unique experiment in architectural pedagogy, the complex in Scottsdale was from the start a residential school, a communal as well as an architectural experiment. Perhaps that is one reason Taliesin West has been slow to accrue the recognition it deserves as a great architectural site. Little of Wright's work lends itself to easy imitation, but Taliesin West is even more difficult to pigeonhole. It is really an eccentric community consisting of private quarters for the master, residences for senior fellows, and dormitories for students; communal kitchen and dining facilities; two theaters; offices; workshops; and exterior terraces, gardens, and courts. The uniqueness of Taliesin West was born not only of its site and design but also of its unusual program.

Wright described the buildings at Scottsdale as "barbaric architecture." As few post-industrial age designers have ever been able to do, he created a community of buildings that truly integrates the earth and the sky. The way his buildings marry the earth below and the air above is unprecedented in modern times; the way the build-

ings are a part of the desert seems more mindful of Indian caves than of the comfortable homes that dot nearby streets. His buildings possess a sense of permanence while, strangely, conveying a feeling (no doubt even more pronounced in earlier canvas-topped incarnations) that the place is transitory. Wright succeeded in distilling a sense of the Sonoran Desert and turning it into buildings.

The Richard Lloyd Jones house in Tulsa, Oklahoma.

IV   A CONCLUDING CODA

Richard Lloyd Jones House
David Wright House
Robert Llewellyn Wright House

When this book was conceived, as writer and photographer we sought to explore the thesis that an architect building for himself and, perhaps, for near relations, would have more aesthetic freedom than when building for a client and having to pay due regard to the client's tastes and needs. We hoped that an examination of this particular body of work would provide us with a provocative angle of approach to Mr. Wright. As is usual when examining the work (and life) of Frank Lloyd Wright, we confronted both more and less than we had anticipated.

Mature trees and bushes have softened the lines of the house so the large structure (8,442 square feet, enormous for its day) no longer has quite the same institutional feel.

Happily, our researches produced nothing counter to the notion that Wright, when working for himself, was least encumbered and at his most creative. The Home and Studio and both Taliesins make a *prima facie* case. The same is true of some of his work for relatives, such as the Hillside Home School and the Romeo and Juliet Windmill, built for aunts Nell and Jane Lloyd Jones.

The hypothesis proved less valid when it came to the three houses he built for relatives: Westhope, built for his cousin Richard Lloyd Jones, and the two modest dwellings designed for his sons David and Llewellyn. The correspondence that survives from the time of construction of the first two in particular is as prickly as any that Wright had with unrelated clients. His correspondence with his cousin Richard Lloyd Jones is especially revealing. Wright and Richard had a classic architect-client exchange (or was it architect *versus* client?). There is the flattery, with admiration for Wright's work from one corner, appreciation of the client's good taste from the other. The plans are slow in coming (a consistent pattern with Wright); revisions emerge even more slowly, producing exasperation on the client's part. Wright then becomes outraged when demands are made. Both parties are on the brink of terminating the relationship when amends are made and the partnership resumes. The obligatory tugs-of-war over money follow (Wright needs and wants some, the client says it's too much, a compromise is reached). The client wants a Wright house but only over time comes to realize the risks, expense, and hassles involved.

Wright was rarely easy to work with, despite his charm and wit. He was a visionary who saw clients, money, and tradition as obstacles to overcome.

The first of the three houses he designed for family members was the RICHARD LLOYD JONES HOUSE. Built in Tulsa, Oklahoma, in 1929, this house was designed for a cousin of Wright's on his mother's side. One of the merits of including it in this volume is that its basic material, the textile block, was of Wright's devising and one in which he did some important work but none at his own homes.

The lines of the Lloyd Jones House—vertical rows of masonry alternating with tall strips of windows—are familiar today, resembling the screen walling of countless office buildings. But in its time it was a

very advanced house, in part because it used reinforced block and slab elements in a way that, in the jargon of architectural criticism, directly expresses its structure.

It is not a house that has garnered a great deal of admiration from the critics; it's been described as prison-like and downright ugly. In fact, black-and-white aerial photographs from the time of construction reveal an enormous, institutional-looking structure that seems to be stranded in a great open prairie. The intervening three-quarters of a century has resulted in a much more appealing integration of house and setting. The house is no masterpiece, perhaps, but no longer is it a jarring presence on the landscape.

The house and, in particular, one of its failings led to an inspired remark, made by Mrs. Lloyd Jones to Herbert ("Hib") Johnson, a prospective client of Wright's.

Ever the magician with windows, Wright created an elaborate construct for the entrances to the Richard Lloyd Jones house, a very effective geometric design that breaks up the rigid pattern of alternating bands of vertical windows and masonry piers.

He was scouting Wright's work and, at that time, the Tulsa house was one of Wright's most recent designs. Johnson arrived at the house in a driving rain and discovered the floor inside dotted with strategically placed containers. Each of these vessels had been located to catch copious drips that fell from the leaky roof (another of Wright's trademarks). Mrs. Lloyd Jones commented dryly to Johnson, "This is what happens when you leave a work of art out in the rain." Johnson was undeterred, as he went on to commission a house and the landmark Johnson Wax Administration Building with its unforgettable mushroom columns. (Less memorable, perhaps, was its Pyrex tubing roof which also leaked volumes of water.)

The Lloyd Jones House is more significant than some other lesser works of Wright because of an accident of timing. The commission came along during Wright's great doldrums (in the decade before Fallingwater was built in 1935, less than a handful of his designs were built, none of them major works). In retrospect, this period of enforced idleness may have been a useful time for Wright: not only did the plan for the Fellowship emerge, but his personal style underwent a transformation. Taken as a single work, the Lloyd Jones House may well have been less than a success; considered as an étude, it looms large. It features vestigial traces of the

The David Wright House, the design that Wright memorably labeled, "How to live in the southwest."

prairie style, but one can see elements also of the nascent Usonian house in the buttress-like stacks of concrete blocks.

Built for his fourth child, the DAVID WRIGHT HOUSE dates from 1950. Located just outside Phoenix, the house was David's home for almost half a century (his widow, Gladys, was still in residence when these pictures were taken).

The story is told that FLLW took a seat in his office one morning at Taliesin West to design the house. He made one freehand sketch of the general plan on a sheet of tracing paper and noted some dimensions on the right side of another sheet in red pencil. Then, working with a compass and triangles, he drew a floor plan, two elevations, a section with room heights and floor levels, and added various handwritten notes. The work required forty-five minutes. He signed it with a flourish: "How to live in the S.W. Mar. 3/50. FLLW."

The story is at least partly apocryphal: The house didn't quite leap full blown from his imagination, as FLLW had been working on cyclone shapes for years for the Guggenheim Museum, and in reality the David Wright house was almost certainly a recycling of an earlier unbuilt design that had been commissioned by a client in New Jersey. But the adaptations FLLW made to the peculiarities of the site made it work. The plot was an orange grove outside Phoenix with a backdrop of mountains. He moved the living areas to the second level

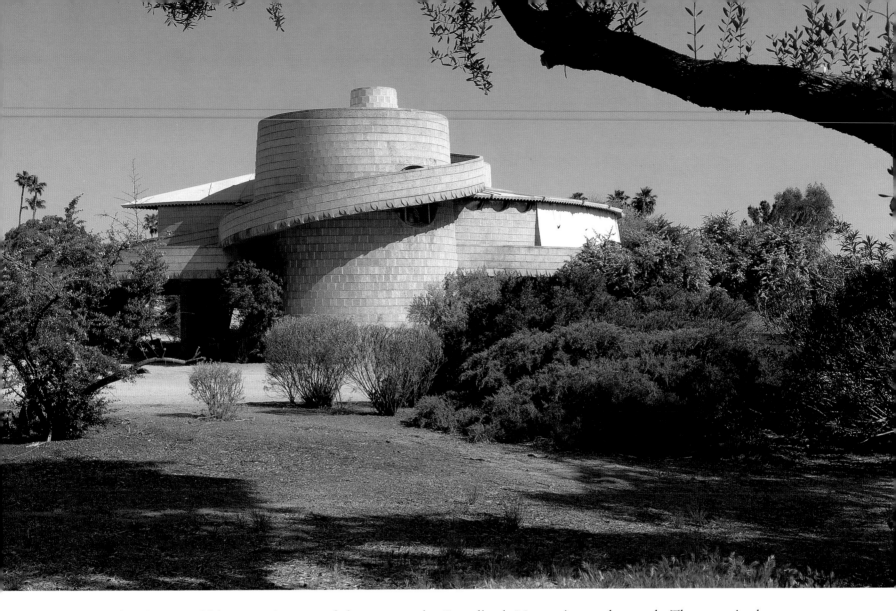

so the view would be over the tops of the trees to the Camelback Mountains to the north. The ramp is also a garden, as is the lower level which, by providing shade and encouraging breezes, helps cool the living space in Phoenix's hot climate. While the preliminary sketches were by Wright, the working drawings were done by an apprentice.

Wright was well known for his disregard of his client's wishes; even when dealing with family members he maintained the same I-know-what's-good-for-you attitude. As originally conceived, the house was to be built of wood; Wright, intent more on his vision than on his client-son's talents and predilections, left it so. But David Wright, who retained through the decades a residual bitterness at his father's abandonment of the family,

was more independent than most FLLW clients. He built the elevated, semicircular house and its spiral ramp of concrete block (he was, after all, an engineer and a concrete executive). Another man, a different sort of father, might have gone to the trouble of adapting his design to his son's expertise. But David Wright had learned at age fourteen how to get along without his father, so he, along with Taliesin fellow Wesley Peters (who was then married to David's half-sister), reconfigured the house using block. Most of it was stock block, though the decorative frieze was made to order. In a sense, it's less remarkable that the father's design had more to do with his own desire to see an unbuilt work come to be than that the son asked for it at all. FLLW's work consistently took precedence over family obligation

The entrance façade of the Robert Llewellyn Wright house.

Like his brother David, Robert Llewellyn Wright was not an architect (unlike brothers John and Lloyd). He eventually asked his father to design him a home.

He was FLLW's sixth and last child by his first wife, Catherine, and was remembered by the other siblings as their father's favorite. Llewellyn's hemicycle house–FLLW's word for his almond-shaped designs–was built in Bethesda, Maryland, just outside Washington, D.C., where Llewellyn Wright practiced law, alternately working for the Justice Department and in private practice.

Executed in 1953, the ROBERT LLEWELLYN WRIGHT HOUSE is two stories tall, built of concrete block and wood. Its design nicely represents the Usonian houses. It is a compact house, intended to be modest in cost, but elevated above the average house of the time thanks to thoughtful design.

While the final plans are known to have been executed by Taliesin fellows, the unmistakable stamp of FLLW can be seen in the conception and especially the siting of the house. The house seems to have been lowered into the steep slope of the property, its prow overlooking the dense vegetation. The angular topography gives it a sense of isolation, despite its setting in a well-developed suburban neighborhood.

Frank Lloyd Wright died at Taliesin West in April of 1959, after a brief stay in a Phoenix hospital. His remains were driven back to Wisconsin for burial in the Unity Chapel graveyard. Wright was mourned by Olgivanna,

his children, and his inner circle–by those who survive, he still is–but his demise did nothing to diminish his reputation.

To an extent that even the supremely confident Frank Lloyd Wright could hardly have anticipated, his fame and reputation today have taken on a golden glow. His gifts as an architect, designer, and even philosopher are widely recognized. Wright sites enjoy growing visitation, licensed products proliferate, and his life has been celebrated on PBS by Ken Burns. Many of his buildings have been recognized by national and international organizations as treasured monuments. His legacy is that of a certifiable cultural icon.

Wright's contributions to the art of architecture have proven varied. He devised or adapted for residential architecture a wide array of technical innovations. The list includes casement windows, plate glass, corner windows, and increased fenestration; early air conditioning, radiant heating, and fireproofing strategies; foundations on grade without cellars, concrete block, reinforced concrete cantilevers; and extensive use of built-ins, open plans, radial plans, broad

The citrus grove still remains around the base of the seventy-seven foot radius of the David Wright house, though the neighborhood is now suburban.

As with the David Wright house, the plans at the Robert Llewellyn Wright house had to be adapted, in this case to reduce costs. Yet the signal element of the house, the prow, is stylishly finished with wood screws and scarfed joints.

roof overhangs, carports, and attic-less houses. His influence went beyond buildings: in fact, design in the twentieth century–in particular, interior design and the decorative arts–was perhaps even more influenced by his work than was architecture.

Quantifying his influence is not the task here. Rather, our purpose has been to seek some understanding of the man and his work by examining what he chose to build for himself and his family. It has proven possible to see Wright's work at the Oak Park home and the two Taliesins as inevitable. That

Compliments of FLLW and the Fellowship, a design was made for a pecan-shaped footstool and coffee table to complement the shape of the house.

is a biographical construct, of course, a convenient means of organizing the facts and themes of Wright's life into a sort of architectural time line. But it's an approach that Wright, the man who made his own myths, might find congenial.

To examine carefully the Home and Studio–in a sense, to decode it–is to better understand the birthing of suburban style. The inspiration for Taliesin, the noble country villa that anchors the middle period of Wright's work, was borne of Wright's happy days with Mamah Borthwick Cheney in Tuscany and, much earlier, his youthful summers on the Lloyd Jones farms. Digging through the layers of Taliesin allows a better understanding of the works of his middle years. Wright was 65 when he published his *Autobiography*, milestones that for many people signal an acceptance that the time has come for summing up. But that same year, Wright and Olgivanna launched the Taliesin Fellowship and, in the years thereafter, rejuvenated his nearly dormant practice. He conceived the affordable and modular Usonian house; he built his most memorable and

Usonian houses were typified by low ceilings, central fireplaces, and modular construction. In this view of the main room of the Robert Llewellyn Wright house, kitchen and dining facilities fill one end of the elongated space.

best-loved building, Fallingwater; he designed the surprising Johnson Wax Administration Building; and he conceived his urban dream, Broadacre City.

Then came Taliesin West, his unique desert campus. That unprecedented complex anticipated the elder Wright who, heady with late-life success, allowed his imagination to run free. His freeform experiments at Taliesin West surely helped him as he designed a museum in the form of a cyclone and adapted a range of geometric shapes and "organic" forms in new and expressive ways. One can take such musing too far–Wright's was not a life with a rigid internal coherence–but there is an almost architectural play of movement to the sequence of his designs.

Another appeal of his three houses is that they come complete with a fourth dimension. Unlike many of his designs, which are usually seen as the work of a fixed moment (typically the time of design and construction), neither the Home and Studio nor the Taliesins were static during Wright's habitation. As we have seen in

looking at each of them, there was a never-ending series of attempts to try something new and different. One of Wright's greatest attributes was his refusal to stand still, his willingness to risk untraveled territory. His risk ratio–if there is such a statistic–would have been off the actuarial charts. His work was always in motion. He revisited good ideas again and again. Even at the end of his life, his imagination remained restless, his eye remarkably fresh and curious.

Nor is the appeal of these places perfection: Not everything works. But the trials (and the errors) are part of the charm. Just as Thomas Jefferson tinkered with Monticello for forty years, Wright tried out his latest notions at the Taliesins for a half a century. (It is intriguing that Jefferson's experimental roofs always leaked, too.) Both Taliesins are imperfectly constructed. In its tough winter climate, Taliesin was never thoroughly weatherproofed (even today, there are gaps between masonry elements wide enough to put your fingers through). Taliesin West is no different; a maintenance crew is forever at work patching and fixing. Yet their shabby casualness conveys a feeling for the improvisation that was always in the air when Wright was there.

At the Robert Llewellyn Wright house, the multi-purpose common room at the core of the home features numerous space economies, including a built-in desk, bookshelves, and other accessories that leave room for a piano at center.

Longtime fellows laugh off the leaky roofs, settlement problems, failed radiant heating systems, and the like as small matters. Wright really had his eye on posterity, on the future.

In *Frank Lloyd Wright: His Life and His Architecture*, the best Wright biography, author Robert C. Twombly wrote, "Making the avant-garde accessible was part of Wright's genius." That insight must be qualified, as Wright, as we have seen him in his homes, was no modernist. He talked about the machine but he didn't build machines for living. At heart he was more

Deteriorating blocks and another leaky roof . . . hallmarks of limits tested.

nearly a romantic, an admirer of artists and craftsmen, a believer in animal instinct, a man of environmental inclination. He built organic buildings, looking to the principles of nature to guide him, to build with nature rather than against it. The Home and Studio looked inward; Taliesin looked out; Taliesin West looked up. The low roof lines of Taliesin with their projecting eaves shielded the place; the translucent, flapping canvas of Taliesin West incorporated the life of the desert into the buildings.

Perhaps it is fitting to end with Taliesin West. The complex is a quiet presence, dominated by the colors and vegetation of the desert in the foreground and the mountains on the horizon. Having been there, a visitor will find it impossible to imagine what the landscape would look like without it. In the same way, it is hard to imagine American architecture in the twentieth century without Frank Lloyd Wright.

Wright's gravestone at the Unity Chapel graveyard in Spring Green. (Note, however, that his remains are no longer there, Olgivanna having moved them to Arizona to be with hers.)

NOTES AND ACKNOWLEDGMENTS

As the text of this book was researched in about equal measure by reviewing the vast Wright literature and by visiting sites and talking to those who know them best, the acknowledgments and the notes on sources for this volume must be of a piece. That conjunction is only enhanced by the oral nature of Wright's world–he loved to talk and, equally, loved to be talked about.

To begin, we extend our appreciation to the cooperative men and women at the various places we visited. They include: executive director, Joan B. Mercuri, Gloria Garafalo, Jean Louise Guarino, and especially archivist Fran Martone, all of the Frank Lloyd Wright Home and Studio Foundation in Oak Park, Illinois; the ever-patient and immensely helpful Beth Mylander of Taliesin Preservation, Inc., for her time and insight into Taliesin in Spring Green, Wisconsin; Suzette Lucas, director of external affairs for the Frank Lloyd Wright Foundation, for her help at Taliesin West; and Margo Stipe and Indira Berndtson in Scottsdale at the Frank Lloyd Wright Foundation Archives. And to the Frank Lloyd Wright Home and Studio Foundation for permission to reprint the floor plan that appears on page 27; to Taliesin Preservation, Inc., for the floor plan of Taliesin on page 65; and the Frank Lloyd Wright Foundation for the Taliesin West plan on page 115.

At the Taliesin Fellowship, longtime Taliesin fellows Bruce Brooks Pfeiffer, Cornelia Brierly, Tom Casey, Susan Jacobs Lockhart, and Frances Nemtin were all most generous with their time for interviews and offered key insights into Mr. Wright's days in residence at the Taliesins.

Among Wright descendants, thanks go to Richard Llewellyn Wright's sons, Timothy K. Wright and Thomas L. Wright, for their helpful conversations, and especially to Thomas for his patience while we photographed what is now his domicile. Our appreciation, too, to Eric Lloyd Wright for helpful guidance and insights; to Gladys Wright, widow of David, who reluctantly talked in brief of her husband's complicated relationship with his father; and to Florence L.J. Barnett, daughter of Richard Lloyd Jones, who was much more forthcoming and proved helpful in understanding the construction and subsequent history of Westhope.

Over the years, many people have fed our Wright enthusiasm. Though necessarily a partial list, among those helpful Wrightians are Linda Waggonner at Fallingwater; Thomas Monaghan; John O'Hern; John I Mesick; Sara-Ann Briggs, executive director of the Frank Lloyd Wright Building Conservancy; and Donald P. Hallmark, director of the Dana-Thomas House in Springfield, Illinois, who is a fount of wisdom on Wright and always willing to help.

Our appreciation, too, to David Morton, senior editor of architecture, at Rizzoli International Publications, Inc., who contracted for this book, to Jonathon Fairhead and Damon Ferrante of Rizzoli, and to Emma Sweeney of Harold Ober Associates, Inc., who placed the book and, along with Dominck Abel, represented our interests.

Now to the literature. The following is not intended to be a comprehensive Wright bibliography; that ground has been well covered by other researchers. The sources cited are those that proved most valuable in the preparation of *Wright For Wright*.

Many hours were invested in the archives at the Home and Studio and at Taliesin West examining primary source material, including drawings, photographs, and Wright's voluminous correspondence. Historic

Structures Reports for the Home and Studio and Taliesin also were invaluable.

Wright's own *An Autobiography* (1932) was another important source, in particular for the inspiration that produced Taliesin. Wright left much else for consideration, virtually all of it to be found in *Frank Lloyd Wright Collected Writings, Vol. 1–5*, Bruce Brooks Pfeiffer, editor. (New York: Rizzoli International Publications., Inc./Frank Lloyd Wright Foundation, 1991, 1992, 1993, 1994, 1995). A number of memoirs offered additional perspectives, including Cornelia Brierly's recent *Tales of Taliesin* (Tempe, Ariz.: Arizona State University/Frank Lloyd Wright Foundation, 1999); *Years with Frank Lloyd Wright: Apprentice To Genius* by Edgar Tafel (New York: Dover Publications, Inc., 1979); *My Father Who Is On Earth* by John Lloyd Wright (New York: G. P. Putnams's Sons, 1946); and *About Wright: An Album of Recollections by Those Who Knew Frank Lloyd Wright*, Edgar Tafel, editor (New York: John Wiley & Sons, Inc., 1993).

There is a remarkable range of secondary sources. Among the classic essays are those by Vincent J. Scully, Jr., *Frank Lloyd Wright* (New York: George Braziller, Inc., 1960) and *In the Nature of Materials: The Buildings of Frank Lloyd Wright 1887–1941* by Henry-Russell Hitchcock (New York: Da Capo Press, originally published in 1942). More recent writings include Neil Levine's invaluable *The Architecture of Frank Lloyd Wright* (Princeton, N.J.: Princeton University Press, 1996). Another standard reference is *The Frank Lloyd Wright Companion* by William Allin Storrer (Chicago: The University of Chicago Press, 1993) which along with his earlier *The Architecture of Frank Lloyd Wright: A Complete Catalog* (Cambridge, Mass.: MIT Press, 1974, 1978) constitute something of an atlas to Wright's work. An intriguing interpretive look at Wright is to be found in *The Wright Space: Pattern and Meaning in Frank Lloyd Wright's Houses* by Grant Hildebrand (Seattle, Wash.: University of Washington Press, 1991). Numerous back numbers of *The Frank Lloyd Wright Quarterly*, published by the Frank Lloyd Wright Foundation, proved useful, as did a wide range of periodical articles. One in particular bears special mention, the widely republished essay *A Walk through Taliesin* by architecture critic Robert Campbell.

When it comes to biographies, there is Brendan Gill's irreverent but highly readable *Many Masks: A Life of Frank Lloyd Wright* (New York: Random House., Inc., 1987). It is an excellent antidote to the more worshipful volumes, though, again, Robert C. Twombly's *Frank Lloyd Wright: His Life and His Architecture* (New York: John Wiley & Sons, 1979) remains the best primer to the buildings.

Last but hardly least, our special appreciation goes to this book's designer, Doris Straus, who was very much a partner in assembling this volume, taking our words and pictures and melding them into a unique and uniform whole.

INDEX

Page reference in **boldface** indicate the page number of an illustration or its caption.

Art Center College of Design
Library
1700 Lida Street
Pasadena, Calif. 91103